SUN, STORM,
AND
SOLITUDE

SUN, STORM, AND SOLITUDE

DISCOVERING HIDDEN ITALY

ON THE

CAMMINO DI SAN BENEDETTO

KARL KEATING

RASSELAS
HOUSE

Published by Rasselas House
El Cajon, California
RasselasHouse.com

Cover design and formatting by Damzonza.com

ISBN 978-1-942596-39-4 Ebook
ISBN 978-1-942596-38-7 Paperback

Contents

Who, What, Where 1

Arrivals 21

The Open Road. 35

The Saint of Lost Causes 51

A Chariot and Wise Admonitions 63

Life on the Farm 77

Lost and Found. 89

Momentarily in the Sierra. 101

You Can't Get There from Here 111

Ghostly Houses. 123

Rise Up and Walk. 135

Places Seen and Unseen. 145

Medieval Streets 161

Misplaced Trust 173

Homage to a Mandolin Maker 183

Where All Roads Lead. 195

Gratitude 207

WHO, WHAT, WHERE

I STOOD AT THE recalcitrant kiosk. After much fussing it read my passport, but instead of spitting out my boarding pass it kindly informed me that my flight had been canceled.

I had been at the airport all of ten minutes.

An American Airlines representative motioned me to the end of a long and immobile line. I had two hours until the Flight That Was Not to Be, a flight that would have given me enough time to catch the transatlantic flight leaving Dallas, but DFW was closed. Thunderstorms, they said. Nothing was going in or out. I berated myself for not having thought things through when making my reservation. I didn't have to go through Dallas. I didn't have to take American. I should have remembered that Dallas, while under no threat from hurricanes or snow in May, is cursed with being situated in a vast plain through which thunderstorms roll with monotonous regularity. Almost any other layover city would have been a safer choice.

The words "God is against me" came into my mind. It was a line from near the end of Whittaker Chambers' autobiography,

Witness. He was at the vortex of a nationally-important legal battle and had just been told something that seemed to destroy his veracity. Me? I was on my way to Italy to hike. *Non é impor-tante* is what Italians would say of what I was up to, but at the moment, after so many weeks of preparation, after so many more hours than expected to get my gear chosen and packed, there I was, going nowhere except, apparently, home.

Was God against my going on this pilgrimage, which was at once more and less than a pilgrimage? Was this a last-minute sign that I should have stayed home and tended to domestic affairs: the dozen small repairs that I had put off for months, the backpacking book manuscript that had been languishing since John Muir last hung up his hiking boots, the tax returns that were on extension?

After fifteen minutes of frustrating immobility, the line began to move, other clerks opened other windows, and shortly I was speaking with an overworked woman who, as she took my passport, was interrupted by a customer whose anger should have been directed at the clouds above Dallas rather than at her. Before I could tell him to butt out and get in line, she directed him elsewhere, and he moved off with the air of a man who thinks he is owed much.

"I can route you through Philadelphia," the rep said to me. "You'll arrive in Rome two hours later than you otherwise would have."

"I'll take it," I said, realizing that God wasn't against me but was giving me a lesson in patience. I had been scheduled to land in Rome around 7:00 a.m. Landing at 9:00 a.m. still would let me get to Spoleto early enough to catch the 2:00 p.m. bus to Norcia, where a reservation awaited me at Palazzo Seneca.

On the plane I watched the route map on the seatback screen in front of me. I hadn't flown on American for a while and wondered whether the map recently had been modified and whether any passengers had expressed consternation at its markings.

It was enough that the large-scale map showed cities no passenger ever had heard of. Most Americans can't find Iceland on a map that has an arrow pointing to the island. If they have heard of any Icelandic city, it's Reykjavik. It's understandable that a map showing transatlantic airline routes might show Reykjavik. After all, it has an international airport, and Americans visiting Iceland land there. But the map on Flight 1055 didn't show Reykjavik, which is at the southwest corner of the country. It showed instead Akureyri, which is on the north-central coast. Why Akureyri? It has an airport that is denominated international, but the only international flights seem to be on Icelandic Airlines to Copenhagen. American Airlines doesn't stop there at all, so why is Akureyri on its in-cabin flight map?

More disconcerting were other things on the map: indications of where ships had sunk. Off the coast of Massachusetts was a circle labeled "Thresher 1963." That submarine accident cost 129 lives. Further into the Atlantic were "Titanic 1912" and "Bismarck 1941," each with much greater loss of life. What was the purpose in showing where those ships sank, particularly as flight attendants were demonstrating how to use a life vest "in the event of a water landing"? Shouldn't the mapmakers have suspected that showing where ships went down might be too much for those airline passengers for whom riding in a metal tube at 35,000 feet is fear-inducing anyway? I wasn't one such passenger. I used to fly my own plane and had no fear of flying, but still.

I took up hiking two decades ago. Backpacking too. I spend several weeks each year in the Sierra Nevada wilderness, and I try to get in one or two trips to the bowels of Grand Canyon. I also do a lot of local hiking. I'm blessed to live within easy reach of the Pacific Crest Trail and of mountains that offer good exercise and welcome solitude.

The latter appeals to me particularly. I like people, but I also like being away from people. I like the hurly-burly of everyday life but also the silence and serenity of wilderness. "Only by going alone in silence, without baggage, can one truly get into the heart of the wilderness. All other travel is mere dust and hotels and baggage and chatter." So opined John Muir. He truly went into the wilderness without baggage, just with what he could stuff into the pockets of his greatcoat. Not that hardy, I hoist a backpack and take along more *stuff* than Muir did (but at least my clothing is much lighter than his was, so it probably balances out).

People who learn of my hiking proclivities often ask whether I have hiked "the Camino" and, if not, whether I plan to do so. They mean Spain's Camino de Santiago, which begins in many places but culminates in Santiago de Compostela at the cathedral dedicated to St. James the Greater. I tell them no, and then I tell them why: too many people. More than 300,000 hike the Camino each year, from which fact I have concluded that I would be unable to find solitude as often as I would like.

I admit that the Spanish Camino passes through areas that would interest me—but not enough such areas for me to make the effort to see them. Whenever I say that, I have in mind Samuel Johnson's reply to James Boswell when the latter told him about the Giant's Causeway, a geological oddity on the northern coast of Ireland similar to the basalt columns of Devil's Post-

4

pile National Monument in California. Boswell asked, "Is not the Giant's Causeway worth seeing?" Johnson replied, "Worth seeing? yes; but not worth going to see."

That, I confess, is my perception of northern Spain. It is worth seeing and worth hiking through but not, so long as there are other places higher on my list of places to see and to hike, worth going to see and going to hike—at least not for me. That and the crowds.

I have been to Spain, and I like the country. I have been to Italy more often and like it more, so it was natural for me to take an interest in an Italian cammino. (Note how the spelling changes from Spanish to Italian.) When I heard about the Cammino di San Benedetto, which honors and follows the life of the founder of Western monasticism, I thought it was worth investigating. When I learned that it was a newish route that sees only about one percent of the Spanish route's hikers, I suspected I would find along it welcome solitude, not to mention historical, cultural, and religious encouragement.

My plan was to make two trips, one in December and one the following May. The first would be a driving tour of the Cammino di San Benedetto, to get the lay of the land (at least the part that could be driven) and to meet and interview some of the people along the way—and some who were out of the way. Having a car would allow me to visit spots unrelated to the Cammino and to visit friends, old and new, who lived a distance from it. Then I would return in May to walk the entire route. Such was the plan. As it turned out, I was unable to return to Italy the following May and had to wait for May of the next year. Not only did that put my plans a year behind schedule, but I missed hiking in a May that apparently was pleasant and instead hiked in a May that thought it belonged to winter rather than to spring.

On that December trip, when I went to meet Simone Frignani, the creator of the Cammino di San Benedetto, the motorway took me not far from Ravenna. I made a detour with a narrow purpose: to visit the tomb of Dante Alighieri. I had been in Ravenna before, taking in the major sights, but one sight eluded me, Dante's tomb. It was closed for renovation—not only closed but entirely sealed behind tall and opaque construction fencing.

I have been writing, desultorily, a beginner's guide to Dante and thought it right and proper, fitting and just, to pay homage to the world's greatest epic poet, given that I was in his neighborhood. I didn't linger in Ravenna, not having the time. I parked in the Largo Firenze parking lot, grabbing what seemed to be the last spot, and walked around the Basilica of St. Francis to the nondescript corner where Via Dante Alighieri meets Via Guido da Polenta, happily finding the tomb accessible and freshened up. I spoke silently with Dante for a little while and then headed back toward the motorway.

Having a car not only allowed me to see the deceased Dante and the living Frignani but to visit places near the route of the Cammino but not normally reached by pilgrims on foot. I thought it an advantage to have a broad, automobilistic view that would contrast with a later narrow, pedestrian view. I knew that on the hike I would be limited in where I could go—along the trail, certainly, but not far off it, unless serendipity showed me the way, and serendipity is something you can hope for but can't count on.

In retrospect I was grateful to have made the December journey, since the hike in May had its Decembery—or at least wintry—elements. I had chosen May for the mild weather and for the avoidance of summer's humidity. From Southern California,

I have lived almost all of my life in an arid climate, and my body does not deal well with humidity. I expected the hike of the Cammino to be challenging, but I didn't want it to be unnecessarily purgatorial. I don't mind sweating, if I'm exerting myself, but I mind if I sweat even when still. That's what humidity does to me.

I was in Kyoto in October fourteen months before my December tour of the Cammino. It was not a hot October, but for me it was a humid October. I remember sitting in trains, looking at the "salarymen" in their suits, each man dry and composed. I wore a short-sleeve shirt yet dripped sweat. Most days, in the interests of social acceptability, I took two showers. One day I took three. I used to be able to travel to Japan in October without inconvenience, but after that trip I decided to restrict my visits to November or later. I chalked it up to the effects of age.

That meant, for my Italy hike, that I chose May rather than June, fearing that June would prove as humid in Italy as was October in Japan, but this particular May turned out to be no harbinger of summer. Quite the opposite. Halfway through my hike I was told that the month was proving to be the coldest and wettest May in decades.

Some days as I hiked the weather was preternaturally good, the sun bright, the sky clear, the temperatures in my comfort zone, but other days I walked head bowed into stiff, cold winds and through rain so strong that I hardly could see the way ahead of me. Those days I was unable to cover as much distance as I had planned, particularly when the route was mainly along dirt trails rather than paved roads. Inclement weather slowed me down on the roads but forced me to go at far less than half my normal speed on trails that were gooey mud or slick forest duff or wide pools that could be skirted only tediously. More often than

I liked, prudence led me to avoid precipitous and waterlogged trails and to stick to paved roadways. Most of these counted as legitimate Cammino routes—they were the alternates for bicyclists, who in no way could have managed the dirt (or mud) trails—but pavement didn't guarantee speed in bad weather. A few times I happily accepted rides, either to avoid hiking through downpours or to avoid falling even further behind.

Once I got into town—perhaps I should say, into hamlet or village—it usually was so late that I had insufficient time to explore the neighborhood. I missed seeing things the guidebook suggested I ought to see. There were side ventures I wish I could have made, detours I wish I had had time for. I was glad to have caught some of them when I visited in cold but dry December. Someday I will have to return to fill in the lacunae.

The upshot was that, mainly because my May was stormy, I lost time on the hike and wasn't able to walk the entire route, missing the last two (of sixteen) waypoints, Roccasecca and Montecassino. I was grateful that I had visited those places during the earlier trip. I hadn't padded my hiking schedule with "zero days" (a backpacking term). Had my May been an ordinary May, I would have had no trouble finishing the route and getting to Fiumicino exactly on time. I hadn't foreseen that the weather wouldn't follow my every whim. In retrospect, I wish I had scheduled my return flight for three days later. If I finished the Cammino in a balmy May, that would have meant three free days in Rome or elsewhere. If I met weather delays, that would have meant a full if later completion of the hike.

Why was I on the Cammino di San Benedetto at all? I have explained my aversion to crowded trails, my preference for solitude on demand and the resultant silence, and my desire for the liberty to think—which reminds me of a story.

Years ago I was shopping for a new car. I found a model that seemed right, and I went for the obligatory test drive. The salesman was beside me. No sooner did I start the engine than he turned on the stereo. I as quickly turned it off.

"Don't you want to hear how great these eleven speakers sound?"

"No, I'm not going to use them."

"You're not going to use them? Don't you listen to the radio or a CD when you drive?"

"No."

"Then what do you do on a long trip?"

"I think."

There was awkward pause at the passenger seat, as though I had burped loudly when being introduced to the Queen.

As I say, I like silence; I even cherish it. It relaxes the mind, which in turn helps relax the body, even when the body is being exerted strenuously on a rocky, uphill slog. But I could have found solitude and silence on another Italian cammino, so what attracted me to the Cammino di San Benedetto?

It largely was St. Benedict himself.

He was from what the Romans called Nursia but modern Italians call Norcia. In his time it was a small town in the hills a few days' walk from Rome. In our time it is a small town in the hills a two-hour drive from Rome. Benedict didn't come into the world alone. He had a twin sister, Scholastica. They were born in 480 into a prosperous family. Benedict was sent to Rome for his education, there being nothing appropriate in Norcia (as I will continue to refer to his birthplace). His parents expected him to enter a secular profession, but, as a modern biographer, Adalbert de Vogüé, phrases it, he "took offense at the excessively liberal morality of the student environment and decided to leave Rome with the intention of consecrating his life to the service of God."

Benedict seems not to have informed his parents of this sudden change in his status. He headed for the mountains east of Rome, taking along the family nurse, who had been his servant and possibly overseer in Rome. They paused at a hamlet now known as Affile, about fifty kilometers east of Rome. While there, they got by chiefly on the charity of local Christians. One day the nurse borrowed a sieve with which to sift wheat. She dropped it, and it broke in two. She fell to tears, devastated. Benedict, moved by her reaction, prayed for her and obtained the miraculous repair of the sieve. It was his first miracle. He would go on to perform many more before dying in 547.

Word of the miracle quickly spread, and local people flocked to Benedict. Fearing their adulation, in secret he left Affile and his nurse and went off by himself, northward to nearby Subiaco, where he found refuge in a cave high on the side of a cliff overlooking a deep valley. There he lived for three years, at a level of solitude far beyond what I, fond as I am of solitude, could endure. The only person aware of Benedict's presence was Romanus, a monk whose monastery was on the top of the cliff. He befriended Benedict and periodically lowered supplies to him by rope.

Those three years were the spiritually formative period of Benedict's life. The interlude ended when he was discovered by a local priest and some shepherds. They supported him with food, and he supported them with wise counsel. It wasn't long before the efficacy of his counsel reached other ears. Benedict moved onto the main phase of his life, that of founder of monasteries—a dozen just around Subiaco—and of the longest-lived religious order, which came to be known as the Benedictines. There were attempts on his life by jealous clerics, twice by poison. In each case the attempt was foiled miraculously. At length Benedict's winsomeness, practicality (he once may have lived on a cliffside, but his head was never in the clouds), and evident holiness won over former enemies and attracted innumerable followers. There seems to have been no prissiness or fussiness about him. He was an ordinary man who lived extraordinarily.

At fifty-six airy pages in the Dumbarton Oaks Medieval Library edition, Pope St. Gregory the Great's *Life and Miracles of St. Benedict* is short, with a word count about half again as great as that of Benedict's Rule, which he wrote to guide his monks in their daily lives. Gregory's *Life* in large part is hagiography (chapter titles include "How Benedict made a broken sieve whole and sound," "How he overcame a great temptation of the flesh" [by throwing himself into brambles], "How venerable Benedict revived a boy crushed to death with the ruin of a wall"), but much of what Gregory presents is simple reporting.

He recounts Benedict's youth and early studies in Rome, how he received a monk's habit, how he lived for three years in the cave at Subiaco, how he oversaw the construction of monasteries there, how a jealous monk gave him a poisoned loaf that was stolen away by a raven (we aren't told what happened to the raven), how Benedict was able to read the secret thoughts of a proud monk, how Benedict came to write his Rule, and how he prophesied the date of his own death. Many of Gregory's chapters are short accounts of miracles performed by Benedict, lots of them cures.

Biography in the modern sense didn't yet exist. The first modern biography was Boswell's *Life of Samuel Johnson* (1791). Of course there were biographical writings that long predated Boswell's—Plutarch's *Parallel Lives*, for instance, and *The Lives of the Caesars* by Suetonius, but they weren't biographies as we know them. In Gregory's time and for centuries later there were accounts of the lives of saints, not so much to give "facts" about their lives but to inspire readers in holiness. Much later came Giorgio Vasari's *Lives of the Artists* (1550), the first substantial account of the lives of secular, rather than religious, men. Vasari's work, like that of Plutarch and Suetonius, not to mention the work of the Christian hagiographers, was still something less than what we have come to expect in true biography.

To what extent should a modern reader, or a modern pilgrim along the Cammino di San Benedetto, accept Gregory's account of Benedict's life, particularly the miraculous elements? Gregory was born seven years before Benedict died. We don't know how he amassed most of the information he recounts about his subject, though it is likely he came to know people who had known Benedict and other people who had known people who had known Benedict. Some of the former may have been eyewitnesses to Benedict's miracles, which seem to have been numerous.

In those centuries, oral history was the chief history, since written history was time consuming and expensive to produce. Pride was taken in passing on, intact and without embellishment, what one had been taught. There is no sufficient reason to think that Gregory was misled in most of the facts and incidents he reported about Benedict, Gregory himself being an immensely learned man, and truly learned men know when to be suspicious of what they are told.

So what about, in particular, the many miracles attributed to Benedict, especially miracles of healing, even raising people from the dead? For my part, I have no reason to hesitate in accepting them, absent evidence to the contrary. We know from the book of Acts that the apostles performed similar miracles with regularity. There is nothing to indicate that the power given to them could not be given, here and there in later centuries, to others such as Benedict. Several times Gregory reports how Benedict was able to know men's secret thoughts—just as, in our own time, Padre Pio was said to do, and some of those whose secret thoughts Padre Pio revealed are still alive, having repeatedly told reporters what happened to them when they went to the friar for confession. (It must be an unnerving experience to have your sins told not by you to a priest but to you by a priest.)

All that said, I realize that most who walk the pilgrimage route named after the saint from Norcia not only know little to nothing about his life and work, beyond that fact that he established monasteries, but they also would look askance at much of what Gregory had to say and what Benedict is said to have done. Either they never have given real thought to the possibility of the miraculous or they think that the existence of Science (with a capital S) implies the impossibility of miracles. I find that a strange and fundamentally unreasonable position, but I know it is the position of most people, perhaps even most who walk the Cammino. Yet they walk it. Not a few, I suspect, return home with premonitions of the supernatural that they had not had before beginning their journeys.

It is a pity that the art of biography came centuries too late for Benedict. Gregory the Great's treatment of him provides the basics of his life, with emphasis on the miraculous encounters, but anyone reading it will wish that Benedict had had his Boswell. Benedict himself could not have intuited that it would be he, more than anyone else, who would lay the groundwork for the resurrection of Western civilization. The last Roman emperor, Romulus Augustulus, had been deposed just four years before Benedict's birth, which meant Benedict lived at the beginning of the half-millennium that historians, rather unfairly, call the Dark Ages. However dark the succeeding centuries may have seemed to be, Benedict's work was a bright light that persisted through those years and into our own era.

In an essay he wrote for *Commonweal* in 1952, Whittaker Chambers said, "The briefest prying must reveal that, simply in terms of history, leaving aside for a moment his sanctity, St. Benedict was a colossal figure on a scale of importance in shaping the civilization of the West against which few subsequent figures could measure. And of those who might measure in terms of historic force, almost none could measure in terms of good achieved."

That's my sense. I find Benedict fascinating and what he accomplished, historically speaking, nearly incomprehensible. Most people who lived when he lived were unaware that their civilization was in collapse. When civilizations collapse, they usually do so slowly, even quietly. People going about their everyday lives perceive troubles but they don't perceive overall civilizational decline. But Benedict and a few others of his time noticed, and their actions produced, in the long run, a new civilization that only in our era has reached a level of exhaustion similar to that of the Roman civilization of Benedict's era.

I chose to hike the Cammino di San Benedetto partly in homage to Benedict and his accomplishments but for other reasons too. I wanted to see an Italy I hadn't seen before. I wanted to get away from the cares of quotidian life. I wanted sustained, healthy exercise. And I looked for the novelty of the unknown and the unexpected. I found some of each and too much of some.

When we think of pilgrimage routes, the first to come to mind is Spain's Camino de Santiago. For English speakers of a literary bent the next up might be the pilgrimage to Canterbury Cathedral and St. Thomas à Becket's shrine as recounted in Chaucer's *Canterbury Tales*. Or maybe the image is one of the many routes to the Holy Land or to Rome. All these routes have one thing in common. All of them are old—at least as old as the Middle Ages and perhaps as old as Christianity itself. If we wonder who might have been the first to lay out these routes, a little reflection tells us that they grew organically. None of them had a founder, but the Cammino di San Benedetto does. His name is Simone Frignani.

A teacher by profession—his charges range in age from eleven to fourteen—Simone lives not far from the headquarters of Ferrari and about fifty kilometers from Bologna, which itself is a four-hour drive from Norcia, where the Cammino di San Benedetto begins. His university studies were in biology and theology, the last degree being obtained when he was in his forties. Before entering teaching he ran a travel agency in Sassuolo. When I visited him a year and a half before my walk, he pointed out the empty storefront where his shop used to be.

More than a decade ago, Simone found himself faced with seemingly intractable personal problems and sought solace in walking. "I needed a strong contact with nature," he told me. Walking helped him find an explanation for what had befallen him. A visit to Mt. Athos gave him encouragement. The year after that, in 2009, he heard a priest preach on Luke 5, which includes the story in which Christ instructs Simon Peter to lower his net, after a fruitless night of catching nothing. "They took a great quantity of fish, so that the net was near to breaking." Simon Peter, astonished, turned to Christ. "Leave me to myself, Lord, he said; I am a sinner."

"I thought these words were for me," said Simone, who shares the first pope's birth name. "My life started again." The idea for the Cammino di San Benedetto came to him. He felt he knew what he was called to do. He started by reading Gregory the Great's short life of Benedict. He learned where Benedict had been—where he was born, where he spent his formative years, where he traveled, where he died.

Simone procured topographic maps and started plotting out the future Cammino's stages, choosing paths that Benedict himself might have trod. For the daily stages he aimed for an average length of twenty kilometers and an average elevation gain of four hundred meters. Beyond that, the villages the route would pass through would have to be interesting in themselves. For two years he scouted out trails, clearing out overgrown ones and creating new ones where none existed. He developed friends wherever he went, and many of them assisted in the trail work. He worked with locals to provide lodging for pilgrims and in doing so began to help reinvigorate small towns that had been in decline.

The first edition of *Il Cammino di San Benedetto* was published in 2012. At first there was only the Italian edition, which sold fewer than five hundred copies the first year. It was a modest start. Not a few of the hikers turned out to be German, so a German translation was produced in 2014. By 2017 over 5,000 copies of the two versions had been sold. That September the English edition appeared. The guidebook is now in its fourth edition. It provides explanations of churches visited, ruins unearthed, and pageantry still maintained. Full-page essays recount the lives of saints met along the way: Benedict himself, of course, but also Rita of Cascia, Giuseppe of Leonessa, Francis of Assisi, Thomas Aquinas, and more. Other essays give background on the Benedictine, Carthusian, and Cistercian religious orders, the formation and architecture of monasteries, Gregorian chant, and even the Roman road system.

The publisher is Terre di Mezzo ("Middle Earth"), which is based in Milan and produces guidebooks for many pilgrimage routes. Simone is the sole author of four. *Italia Coast to Coast* is about a route that goes from the Adriatic Sea to the Tyrrhenian Sea. Like the Cammino di San Benedetto, this route is of Simone's own invention. He also wrote *La Via Romea Germanica*, about an ancient route that goes from the Brenner Pass to Rome, and *La Via degli Dei*, a 120-kilometer route in the Apennines between Bologna and Florence. He co-authored a guidebook on the Via Francigena, another ancient route; it runs from the border with Switzerland to Rome. That route and the Via Romea Germanica are more than triple the 305 kilometer length of the Cammino di San Benedetto.

The books published by Terre di Mezzo are uniform in format. The maps are particularly well drawn, there are many color photographs, and the text is sufficiently detailed in turn-by-turn directions that one almost could get by without the maps and certainly without help from GPS, but GPS coordinates can be downloaded. On my walking journey I had the GPS waypoints and the digital version of the guidebook on my phone, and I carried a paperback. (I had purchased both the Italian and English paperbacks but took only the English.)

Simone and I spoke in the lobby of my hotel. After explaining the origin of the Benedictine Cammino, he told me about the Amici di San Benedetto, the Friends of St. Benedict, which has about twenty members who live along the length of the Cammino. They oversee maintenance of the route, assist pilgrims, and do what they can to make the Cammino better known—all at their own expense. During my first visit and my later walk I met several of the Amici. On Facebook Simone periodically posts photos and videos of his team fixing up and adding signage to the route. They constantly are walking it, trimming intruding brush, repositioning and adding markers, and occasionally even rerouting sections to minimize travel on pavement. The Cammino must be one of the best cared for pilgrimage routes in Europe. (There is an extensive website about the Cammino, camminodibenedetto.it, which can be viewed in multiple languages, including English.)

I asked about the pilgrims themselves. About eighty percent are Italian, said Simone. That isn't surprising, since much of the Cammino is within a few hours' drive of Rome. What do pilgrims get out of walking, whether the whole sixteen stages as laid out in the guidebook or just a few days' worth of the route? Simone said the most important thing for many of them is friendship. They meet like-minded strangers who soon are not strangers at all. Many seek the Cammino for reasons much like his when he began his walks: to clear their minds, to help right teetering personal lives, to reconsider their vocations. Most do not hike for overtly religious reasons, but all of them inescapably experience religious elements—not surprising, since the route largely is about the life and journeys of history's most famous monk.

For further data I turned to Terre di Mezzo's website, terre.it, where I learned something that would be confirmed for me later, as I walked the Cammino di San Benedetto: most of the pilgrims are not young. Only a quarter of them are under forty. More than a quarter are over sixty. Nearly a third are in their fifties. They cite multiple reasons for hitting the trail. Half say they just like trekking. An equal number say they enjoy being in nature, and nearly as many say they want to discover areas hitherto unfamiliar to them. Four in ten say they hike for cultural reasons. They want to see the Italy of the past. Only a quarter list religious or spiritual motives—perhaps not surprising in a culture now largely secularized.

As I mentioned, I chose to hike in May for climatological reasons. It turns out May is the second-most popular pilgrimage month in Italy, barely behind the surprising front-runner, August. I say surprising because August is notoriously hot in most of Italy. Historically, that was the month that popes left Rome for the slightly cooler air of Castel Gandolfo. I suppose hiking the Apennines in August is better than wilting on the streets of Rome, but in August of the year I hiked, Norcia's daily high temperatures ranged from 86 to 100 Fahrenheit—not what I would term favorable hiking weather. Many Italian hikers have no choice but to hike in August, since that is the traditional holiday month during which factories close. They hike then or they don't hike at all. After May and August, each of which attracts one-fifth of the annual hikers, the next most popular months are April, June, and September. Fewer than ten percent of the pilgrims hike the Cammino di San Benedetto between October and March.

After my hike, it gave me some comfort to learn that only half walk the entire Cammino in one go. Others deliberately choose to hike only a few days' worth (the guidebook has explicit recommendations for partial hikes), and some, like me, plan to walk the whole way but find themselves obstructed by weather, illness, or other unforeseen circumstances.

ARRIVALS

THE LEONARDO EXPRESS got me from Fiumicino airport to Termini Station in the promised thirty-two minutes. The train left on time and arrived on time. The spirit of Mussolini must have been hovering over it. The only hitch was that I forgot to validate my ticket before boarding. When the conductor came to me, halfway through the trip, he scolded me for my negligence. I looked appropriately humbled, and he levied no fine. This had happened to me on previous trips. Like many people rushing for the every-twenty-minutes train that will take them into Rome, sometimes I forget to stamp my ticket. So far indulgent conductors have let me off the hook. At some point I'll make the wrong facial expression or respond too fluidly in Italian, and I'll have to pay up.

I almost had to pay into a different fund at Termini. I stood before a ticket machine, chose English, and entered my destination, Spoleto. I fished in my pocket for a ten-euro note. Before I could insert it into the slot I was interrupted by a middle-aged Italian man who asked me, in English, whether I needed help.

I hadn't been fumbling, and at such an early stage of my pilgrimage I could not yet have looked befuddled, so I gave him a cold glance and said no. He wore a small backpack—a prop? Rome is notorious for its pickpockets, particularly at Termini Station, through which all tourists pass. A regular Italian traveler, heading off on a trip long enough to warrant a backpack, would have been preoccupied with his own journey, not with mine. Besides, most Italians travel with small suitcases, not with backpacks, and this man didn't strike me as a backpacker. I do lots of backpacking in California and Arizona, so I know what backpackers look like, even middle-aged ones. Why wasn't he toting a suitcase instead? Was it because, once having emptied an unsuspecting traveler's pockets, it was easier to stash ill-gotten gains in a backpack than a suitcase, which would have to be laid on the floor and zipped open?

Usually I give people the benefit of the doubt. Often enough I find myself wrong to assume something about a person and learn, too late, that I had been mistaken. But sometimes it takes a positive act of the will not to make a snap judgment. Like the time I was in the supermarket at home.

Going down one of the aisles, I saw a woman using one of the store's complimentary electric carts. She was younger than the man at Termini but at least twice the volume. She probably was on the far side of 400 pounds, so I didn't begrudge her the cart.

When I approached the checkout line, I found she was directly in front of me. With surprising facility she leapt out of the cart and grabbed a large bottle of diet soda from a rack. The cart's basket—it reminded me of the bicycle baskets used by paperboys back when there were paperboys and back when there were newspapers—was stuffed full of only one other item, several bags of the largest available size of potato chips. I think of potato chips as one of the four basic food groups, but she had enough in the basket to last me several months.

I looked from the chips to her bulk and back to the chips. Well, maybe she was planning a party and realized, at the last minute, that she had neglected to buy chips for her guests. Maybe, but then she would have been expecting dozens of guests. Maybe she was planning to hand out the chips as an act of charity, much as I hand out chips and cold drinks to weary hikers along the Pacific Crest Trail, but then I hand out individual snack-size bags, not bags twenty times their size. I gave up and admitted that the volume of chips in the cart's basket likely had a cause-and-effect relationship to her own volume.

So it was with the man at Termini Station. Maybe he was a particularly outgoing and friendly fellow who, with nothing else to do because he enjoyed an early retirement or simply had no job, hovered around ticket machines lending confused tourists a hand. Maybe. But it was more likely that he lent his hand not metaphorically but all too physically to their pockets.

Some years earlier, when I was leading a tour of Rome, I gathered my clients together the evening before we visited the Spanish Steps. I told them how to protect themselves against pickpockets, who would be out in force the next day. "Gentlemen, leave your wallet in your room's safe," I advised. "Take only one credit card and a little cash." I told the women to put into their purses only items they were willing to have disappear by day's end.

I recounted the story of what happened to me, my wife, and my sister-in-law when the three of us were in Rome. We boarded a train for a short trip and stood at the door. At the next stop two

Gypsy women got on. Although the train car was nearly empty, they stood close to my sister-in-law. Suspecting what was going to happen, I had my wife tell her, in Japanese, to move away quickly. She did, and as she did so I told the women, in Italian, to bug off. They scowled at me and got off at the next stop. I asked my sister-in-law to check her purse. She had had it over her shoulder, with the large flap down and her arm resting over the flap. She lifted the flap and was amazed to find that the long zipper underneath had been opened, though nothing had been taken. It happens that fast.

After the visit to the Spanish Steps one of the men sheepishly confessed that he had ignored my admonition. He felt amply able to take care of himself and his wife. The two of them were standing near the foot of the steps when a woman came up to his wife and thrust a rose into her hand. Confused, she tried to give it back, saying in English that she didn't want it. The other woman was insistent and spoke in rapid Italian. The husband intervened and got his wife away. While he was preoccupied with protecting her, he neglected to protect his own pockets. The woman's accomplice walked by and, unnoticed, took his cash. He had been carrying $300 in American currency.

I have these two incidents in mind whenever I visit Rome. It's a pity to suspect the innocent, but pickpockets usually look innocent, and I'm disinclined to be relieved of my valuables before my trip hardly is underway.

At the small station in Spoleto I bought a bus ticket from the smiling woman behind the counter at the bar. The word *bar* is not to be misunderstood. Let me make a comparison.

In Japanese, a *mansion* is not a home like those found in

24

parts of Beverly Hills. A mansion is what Americans call a con-
dominium. My son and his family used to live in a mansion
in Yokohama. For Japan, their lodgings were considered almost
roomy, but I'm quite sure there are no Beverly Hills mansions
that are only 750 square feet, as their mansion was.

In Italy a bar isn't a bar. It's where Italians eat breakfast, the
chief offerings being coffee in multiple forms and pastries baked
fresh. It's also the place—along with *tabacchi* shops—where you
can buy bus tickets. For reasons unclear to me, bus tickets often
are cheaper when purchased in these shops than when purchased
aboard a bus. Since shopkeepers keep a portion of the ticket
price, you might think the bus company would come out ahead
if tickets were purchased from its drivers, but this is Italy, where
such considerations often don't matter.

I waited half an hour for the bus to Norcia. It had its own
fermata a few steps east of the train station's entrance. On a stone
wall I saw my first commercial use of the Cammino di San Benedetto, an oval metal sign for B&B Santa Vittoria, located ahead
on the sixth stage, the one from Rieti to Rocca Sinibalda. The sign
said the B&B provided shuttle service to the Benedictine abbey
in Farfa, a 45-minute drive from Rocca Sinibalda, and to the half-
as-distant San Salvatore abbey. Perhaps there was insufficient
interest in visiting the abbeys. When I later checked, the website
of the B&B was defunct and perhaps so was the B&B.

When the bus pulled up, half a dozen of us boarded—locals,
going part of the way, most of them. The route was familiar to me.
I had driven it on my previous visit to Italy: a thin road winding
through luxurious green valleys, at times passing by rock forma-
tions so fissiparous that it was necessary to construct concrete
overhangs, much like tunnels, that the road passed under, the

overhangs protecting vehicles from rock slides. It struck me that these overhangs would be good places for bicyclists to escape hailstorms or to rest from summer's heat.

I was the only passenger to disembark at Norcia, the stop being around the back side of the *centro storico* at Porta Ascolana. This threw me off. I had expected the *fermata* to be at what I considered to be the front of the old town, just outside the main archway in the fourteenth-century walls. That was the way I had driven in when visiting Norcia nineteen months earlier. It wasn't a way for buses to enter, though. A bus might make it through the archway and have no trouble going down the main but narrow street, but then what? It couldn't make sharp turns into the side streets. To turn around it would have to intrude itself into the main square, which seemed to be compromised even when small cars traversed it. Going around to the back side of the *centro storico* thus may have been a necessity. Given how little foot traffic there turned out to be in the *centro storico*, I supposed that most residents of Norcia lived outside the old walls. For all I knew, where I was dropped off might have been the demographic center of town.

I checked in at Palazzo Seneca. When I was in Norcia the first time, it was the only hotel available. The other accommodations had been damaged—or even destroyed—in the earthquakes of 2016. I was told Palazzo Seneca, fortuitously, had been retrofitted for earthquakes a few years before. It came through without apparent injury. I was shown to room 208, which happened to be the room I was given the previous visit. Good-sized by European standards, it had a private balcony that was walled in. I could see over the wall to distant hills and nearly rooftops, but someone of average height could not have seen anything.

The receptionist invited me to dine at the hotel's Michelin-rated restaurant. I thanked her but knew I would go elsewhere. I ate there on my previous trip. The food was more than fine, as one might expect, but so was the bill. Sitting alone at a large table, with few other diners around me, I felt awkward. This time I would have felt yet more awkward because I carried no proper clothing. Granted, even upscale restaurants in Italy cater to guests in jeans and open-collar shirts, but I had only synthetic hiking pants and similarly synthetic—and obviously hiking-oriented—shirts, and I had brought but one pair of shoes, already-worn trail runners.

After I settled in my room I took a short walk down the main street. Many of its buildings still were boarded up. I lost count of the signs that said the businesses had moved elsewhere in Norcia. There was a ghost-town air to the place. Halfway to the main archway I found a restaurant, Locanda del Teatro, with doors open and menu posted. The place wasn't open for business yet—few restaurants open even as early as 7:00 p.m. for dinner, and an open door doesn't necessarily mean an open restaurant. As I read the menu a man walked out and sat on the neighboring bench. From his attire I took him to be the cook. We exchanged pleasantries, I asked him when the restaurant began serving, and I said I would see him later.

I didn't see him later, though I returned for dinner. I shouldn't have been surprised. The job of a cook is to stay in the kitchen and cook, not to hobnob with diners. When I showed up, early by Italian standards, the maître d' (is that too formal a term under the circumstances?) showed me to a table part way back from the front door. I accepted the assignment but later regretted it. I should have indicated that I preferred to sit near the gaggle of diners in the room at the rear. They surely were not tourists, and perhaps the man didn't want to make a foreigner feel uncomfortable by seating him amid people whose language he likely didn't know. So, for the first half of my time at the restaurant, I ate alone. Later, a man who clearly was a local—he greeted the barman and waiters jovially—sat at the next table over, but his back was toward me so we didn't converse.

The food being good (and too much; I ordered a salad and a pizza, and the pizza extended well beyond the edges of the dinner plate) and the night being young, I resumed my walk. I went to near the archway and found almost no shops open. I went to the other end of the main street, around the corner from the hotel, and stood at the center of the piazza. The large statue of St. Benedict was there, as I remembered it. The basilica carrying his name also was as I remembered it: completely destroyed, except for the propped-up façade. I walked along one side of the church and peered over the broken walls. Had anything been moved, adjusted, or repositioned since my last visit? It was hard to tell. Latticework rose to thirty feet at the front and above crumpled walls, looking less like something for use by stonemasons than an attempt to emulate the modern entrance to the Louvre.

(Google Maps used to label the church as "Basilica di San Benedetto." Now the label reads "Rovine della Basilica di San Benedetto"—"Ruins of the Basilica of St. Benedict." Similarly with other structures in Norcia, such as the nearby "Rovine delle Chiesa di San Francesco.")

Elsewhere around the piazza the town's important buildings were silent—and had been silent since the earthquakes that occurred over several months. The bell tower of the Palazzo Comunale (city hall) was strapped in thick cables, to hold the stones in place until restoration could commence. When might that be? Would it even be in my lifetime? I looked up at the side of the tower, built of rough stone on the interior but smooth stone blocks on the exterior. A wild crack ran from the top of the ground floor all the way to the roof, passing through a round window and sending out tendrils above it. The crack was a zigzag that followed the cement between the blocks. Like so many other buildings in and around the piazza, the tower was cordoned off.

On the other side of the hotel I came across a small square that had work trucks parked in it. The back half of a church dedicated to St. Rita—the flower of Cascia, the next stop on the Cammino di San Benedetto—had collapsed, and now, years later, the debris was being carted off. Was that all that could be done? Was there no intention to rebuild? There likely was no money, but there also may have been no knowledge. These crumpled buildings were constructed centuries ago. When the artisans who erected them died, did they take with them their knowledge of medieval architecture? How few artisans with the requisite knowledge there must be today—and how many are the buildings that cry for their assistance.

My plan was to check out of Palazzo Seneca early, after grabbing the earliest-possible breakfast. Not wanting to head in the wrong direction the next morning, I looked for the first part of the Cammino. I knew it began in Piazza San Benedetto, but I failed to see a sign marking its beginning. The piazza, though nearly a square, is marked off by a dual-lined circle on its pavement. Six dual-lined arms reach out from the center, which features the still-intact statue of St. Benedict.

Standing near the statue, I scanned the piazza's perimeter, looking for the first of the hundreds of Cammino markers I expected to see on my journey. I knew basically the way to go—diagonally across the piazza from the hotel, to the right of the basilica—but I saw no marker or any other indication that here began one of Italy's newest pilgrimage routes. I had to look at the GPS app on my phone to see that in the morning I would cross the piazza and head down Via Mazzini, a narrow street that began with a stable building on one side and the collapsed basilica on the other.

I walked the route as shown on my phone's screen: along the side of the basilica, then left behind it, then a quick right onto Via Roma, which led toward a gate in the wall that surrounded the *centro storico*. The gate turned out to be the one near which the bus from Spoleto had dropped me off. I hadn't recognized it from the other side. Via Roma seemed misnamed. Nearly every Italian town has a Via Roma, just as it has a Via Garibaldi and a Via Mazzini. Although it isn't true that all roads lead to Rome, in most towns the local Via Roma is the road most likely to get you going in the general direction of the capital. Not in Norcia, where Via Roma is a short street—someone needing a cane can walk it in two minutes—that goes from the rear of the basilica to Via Circonvallazione, the road the bus took to circumnavigate the old town.

Outside the gate, the app indicated that I would take a right, go down a slight hill to an intersection, and then cross the intersection onto a narrow, paved road that would make a beeline for several kilometers. I walked part of the way to the intersection and still saw no marker, but I noticed that at the intersection there would be an abrupt change, from the close quarters of the *centro storico* to open farm country. No suburbs here.

Back at the gate, I noticed something that hadn't been present on my earlier visit. Across the road, hugging the left side of a one-lane street and extending for hundreds of feet, was a set of newly constructed shops, all in a uniform style and all connected by a raised boardwalk. The shops were attached to one another, except for gaps where large trees intervened. There must have been twenty shops—and one communal restroom, at the midpoint. I took it that, if the shops had plumbing, the plumbing didn't go beyond having a sink. These were makeshift structures, intended as temporary refuges until the shop owners could see their "real," often centuries-old shops restored. I suspected "temporary" would end up having a different meaning than the one normally given to it by non-Italians.

I returned to the hotel and laid out my gear. It was a ritual I would repeat daily. I spread out everything on the bed and even dumped out the contents of my ditty bag. Already I was seeing things I needn't have brought. At this point they were small things. Later I would conclude I shouldn't have brought a fleece (the puffy jacket could have served its purpose, which was to keep me warm in unheated hotel rooms and, if necessary, even in bed) and that I could have gotten by with one t-shirt instead of two and one long-sleeve hiking shirt instead of two. I brought two of each out of concern that I wouldn't be able to launder sweaty clothes often enough and that clothes washed in a sink might not dry by morning. Each lodging had a radiator on which I could hang wet clothes but, through an Italian custom inscrutable to me, the radiators operated for only a short and undesignated time either at night or early in the morning, if they operated at all.

I left Palazzo Seneca with a backpack that I thought light enough for the trip. Over the years, particularly during the last decade, I have reduced the weight of what hangs off my shoulders and rests on my hips. On the Cammino I carried Ultralight Adventure Equipment's Ohm pack. At home I had weighed it and all of my gear using a sensitive scale. The empty pack weighed 30.7 ounces. Including half a pound of food and two pounds of water, the entire ensemble, as I exited Palazzo Seneca, weighed twenty-four pounds—far more than a normal day pack but then I had to carry (or thought I had to carry) duplicates of some clothing items and dozens of small things that, if needed, might be needed badly. At least I didn't have to carry a tent, sleeping bag, or inflatable mattress.

Some gear I never used or used infrequently. The travel sheet I used once; I could have gotten by without it. The water filter I used once and didn't really need it even then. I had brought it thinking I might have to take water from a stream, but that never occurred. The wind shirt returned home in the same condition it left home. When I needed protection from wind, I also needed protection from rain, which meant I wore my rain jacket. I brought a travel towel, which I had purchased specifically for the trip. I used it once, when I stayed at a convent; even then I could have asked the good sisters for a towel. I had three hats: a wide-brim Tilley to keep the sun off my face and shoulders, a snug-fitting watch cap for inclement weather, and a ball cap with a folding brim. I never used the ball cap. I brought a nifty Bluetooth keyboard with which, on my phone, I could use Google Docs to make notes of my journey each evening, but I never once did so. I carried a small Moleskine notebook and a pencil, and it was in that notebook that my notes ended up residing.

Looking over my gear list later, I found twenty-nine items (out of 120) that I could have left at home. Most of the unnecessary items weighed less than an ounce, but cumulatively the twenty-nine weighed just shy of four pounds, meaning I could have saved one-sixth of the total weight and been on the Cammino at barely twenty pounds. Four saved pounds may not seem like much, but they become noticeable after putting one foot before the other thirty thousand times a day. If that total of 120 items seems formidable, keep in mind that most of them were small and light: clear plastic liner for the backpack, to keep gear dry in a rainstorm (1.5 oz.); first-aid kit (3.0 oz.); lip balm (0.4 oz.); dental floss (0.5 oz.); nail clippers (0.6 oz.); gaiters to keep debris out of my low-cut trail runners (1.0 oz.); compass (0.4 oz.); duct tape, the one item no hiker should be without (0.4 oz.); pocket knife (0.8 oz.); soft case to hold reading glasses (1.0 oz.); ear plugs, which proved a godsend in a noisy hotel (0.1 oz.), half a dozen medications (a few tablets of each), and so on. Experience has taught me that there are unused items that safely can be left behind and unused items that one always ought to carry, just in case.

Soon enough I learned which gear to place near the top of the backpack, which to place in the side pockets, which to place in the pockets of my pants or hiking shorts. The determining factor was the weather, and the weather on this trip usually was bad. I didn't know that yet. I had no premonition of what was to come, meteorologically, while in Norcia or even the next day. I thought I had been given the weather I had counted on.

The Open Road

I was committed. I had paid my bill at Palazzo Seneca, had said my good-byes to echoes of "Buon Cammino!", and had closed the hotel door behind me. I knew the first few steps: to the right, then diagonally across the piazza and around the collapsed basilica to the gate where the bus had dropped me, then a right down the incline to the intersection, at which point—at least in my mind, though not strictly according to the boundaries of the city—I would leave Norcia for the open road.

The open road. I am a man of the West, in this case meaning the western United States. I relish driving for hours along the lonely desert roads of California and Arizona, where, as everywhere in Italy, speed limit signs are suggestions rather than commands. I have driven roads so straight and so long that their far ends disappeared into haze that seemed to lie at the horizon line, where there was no sign of sentient life aside from lizards that waited (some of them fatally long) to dash across the asphalt as though playing dodge ball with my tires, where low scrub was interrupted sporadically by Joshua trees, which, perhaps appropriately, were never seen by the biblical Joshua and aren't trees anyway.

The open road. To many it means escape, but I had no sense of escaping from anything. I had traveled more than six thousand miles by plane, train, and bus to walk in unfamiliar country, but I left behind no process server, no posse, no bounty hunter. No one was looking for me, and no one, other than my wife, knew I had left home. No one aside from her would have noticed or cared. "He's not at Mass this Sunday? Maybe he's on one of his backpacking trips to the Sierra Nevada or Grand Canyon."

The open road. An actual road this time, not a dirt path as on my domestic hikes, though that would come later. The narrow paved strip left the intersection and headed south through the broad Santa Scolastica plain, hills on either side. Named for St. Benedict's twin sister, the plain must have been familiar to the future monk when he was a boy in Norcia in the last two decades of the fifth century. The collapsed cathedral was built over what was reputed to be his and his sister's birthplace. In their time the town would have looked nothing like today's Norcia. It was settled first by the Sabines in the fifth century before Christ. Today the population is less than five thousand; it must have been smaller in ancient times, even during the town's periodic heydays.

Norcia became allied with Rome during the Second Punic War but seems to have retained its independence for two more centuries, when the first Roman buildings appeared. By the eighth century A.D. there was an oratory, and pilgrims came to honor the twin saints, particularly Benedict, considered the founder of Western monasticism. In the ninth century Norcia fell to the Saracens and thereafter declined, its fortunes rising and falling due to political and military events largely beyond its control and to periodic and large earthquakes entirely beyond its control.

The town rests on a slight rise above the plain, at the foot of the Sibillini Mountains, which are part of the Apennines. Most of the peaks rise above 2,000 meters; the tallest, Monte Vettore, rises to 2,476 meters, but there is no great sense of height, the Santa Scolastica plain being broad and the mountains rounded with age. There are said to be wolves and cougars in these mountains, though they must have been far from the semi-populated areas I traversed. No doubt all around me were wild boar. I never saw one, but I think on that first day of hiking I heard one in the bushes to the side of the trail. The huffing grunt is distinctive. Meeting boars was the only worry I had regarding safety, but I was informed that, though most of their senses are acute, they see poorly, and the best thing to do when confronted is to stand stock still. When I heard the grunt, my intention was to climb a tree if I spotted a boar and it spotted me. (With my luck, I'd come across a boar with uncommonly good eyesight.) As it happened, all the trees around me were saplings so thin that a macaque monkey climbing them would have bent them to the ground.

Not long after leaving the intersection and saying farewell to Norcia I came upon a curious sight: tract homes. You don't see tract homes in rural Italy, where nearly every home, *sui generis*, seems to have been built before Washington thought it wise to cross the Delaware. Many Italian dwellings were erected when the fanciest dwellings in the future United States were wikiups and teepees. Americans have trouble grasping the antiquity of common buildings here—and not so common ones.

Years before I paid a visit to Niccolo Capponi, the son of

Count Neri Capponi, at the family's palazzo in Firenze. It had been the family residence for eight hundred years—the same building, with the original walls and floors and ceiling, though I hope not with the original plumbing. Eight hundred years! Back home, we're lucky to get a good hundred years out of a house before it becomes one with the earth, but then most of our houses are tract homes. In the United States tract homes are unremarkable because ubiquitous. In Italy they are unexpected finds.

Here were twenty-two buildings, duplexes and triplexes, situated on two plots of plant-free, tan land. The buildings must have been erected recently, perhaps for those displaced by the earthquakes, and could have been found on many streets of my own San Diego. Perhaps these plots were chosen because of their proximity to the old city, not five minutes' walk away—or was it because across the street was located L'Artigiano dei Salumi Salvatori, where cold meats of every style from salami to prosciutto have been manufactured for forty years? (There are worse justifications for siting new-house construction.)

On a side street was a similar establishment, Il Casale de li Tappi, where meat likewise was prepared in the Norcineria style. I knew of its existence only because a sign on the road I was walking pointed off to the right, and below the sign was the first Cammino marker I had seen since leaving Norcia, a small, dark-brown rectangle featuring a yellow lowercased *b* with a horizontal line through its ascender, to form a cross. I would see variants of this marker throughout my trip, attached to other signs, fence posts, walls, trees, and even staked squirrel-height on the ground.

The open road, which now was single-lane gravel, became more open after I passed alongside the blank walls of a long industrial building. After the junction with Via Meggiana the road undulated left and right between fields of solid green. Had the crops been mature, perhaps vision forward would have been obstructed, but nothing was more than waist high, aside from occasional trees.

I moved steadily toward Popoli, the first of many hamlets I would pass through. The approach was heralded by a faded wooden sign partly obscured by foliage. At the top, in large red letters, was the name of the town, followed by a red heart. Then, handwritten: "*Benvenuti! Per il Cammino di San Benedetto, sempre dritto.*" Always straight ahead. That would prove to be good advice for the whole of my journey. In small letters hidden behind luxuriant grass the sign continued: "In 65 paces, on the left, is a fountain. Go slowly. Here we don't have a hospital and not even a cemetery." The sign ended with a cheery "Buon viaggio!" I wondered whether Popoli was notorious for fatal traffic accidents and imagined the carnage of two farm tractors colliding at twenty kilometers per hour.

Entering Popoli I came first to Via della Spiga on the right, then Via della Chiesa on the left. The chiesa was that of San Pietro. I didn't bother to investigate, not knowing, on this first day, how long the first leg of my trip would take. I wanted to be sure to reach Cascia while the afternoon was young. Had I taken a left, I would have discovered that Chiesa di San Pietro, like so many other churches of its age, had fallen victim to the tremors of 2016. Half the building was rubble. How long would it remain looking like a quarry? How could a village of two dozen houses hope to effect repairs, especially since other buildings had collapsed too?

The houses that still stood along the road stood right at the road; there was no setback. The slightest inattention while driving, a quick look at the map on one's mobile phone, would be enough to drift a few feet to the side, the result being a sheared-off side-view mirror and a long scratch along a house's flank. Most of these houses were constructed when traffic was horse drawn, and the roads were wide enough for two horses to pass one another but not two carriages—or two cars.

After Popoli the road became rutted. It dodged around trees, and in places the foliage was so thick that a car could not have passed without leaves scraping its doors. Half a mile brought me to Piediripa, not the town of that name twenty miles from Ancona near the Adriatic coast but a village large only in comparison with Popoli. It had perhaps three dozen houses. Here the road I was on ended, and I turned right onto Via dei Santi, aiming now for Cascia. At the turn was a fountain, the first I had seen since Norcia—not a decorative fountain, not a fountain with artistry, but a utilitarian dispenser of water, once the hamlet's main source, before indoor plumbing arrived. The water flowed continuously from a faucet and then pooled in a long, low trough, where horses had been watered.

Shortly before the fountain was a stone house partly collapsed. It was impossible to tell whether the collapse had come from the recent earthquakes or from long neglect. It was a three-story house, but each story was short. There could not have been much headroom in any of the rooms, which made me think the house was constructed centuries ago, when people were half a foot shorter than they are today.

I left farm country, or at least wide fields, aiming for a pass where low hills on the right and left bowed to one another. The fields became fewer and smaller and were hidden behind unkempt bushes that grew alongside the way like hedges, although their existence must have been accidental rather than intentional. Every so often there was a break in the bushes and a locked gate blocking entrance to a field. The lusher fields lower on the plain must have had some means of irrigation—wells, perhaps. There could have been nothing comparable here, higher up; the fields must have relied on the rains, thus limiting choice of crops.

Along the way I came to a recent monument. The road here was dirt and winding. It ran through a narrow valley, low trees covering the hillsides, grass everywhere else. Next to the road was a large rock, what geologists might call an erratic, but true erratics are left in place by retreating glaciers, and I don't know whether glaciers reached this far south in the last ice age. Perhaps this rock just rolled down a neighboring hill when undermined by runoff.

However that may have been, atop the rock was a tomb-stone-like marker. At its apex was the reproduction of a photograph of a smiling, white-bearded man, Luigi Mancinelli. His dates were 1956-2017. Beneath was the benediction: "In memory of a friend who remains always in our hearts. With affection, the Friends of Hunting."

Who was this Luigi Mancinelli? Could he have been the great-great-grandson of the cellist and composer of the same name, who died in 1921? Not likely, I supposed, since that Mancinelli was from Orvieto. More probably this Mancinelli was a local who was highly skilled in hunting wild boars and other game. Perhaps he was the long-time president of the area's hunting club. Perhaps he supplied L'Artigiano dei Salumi Salvatori and Il Casale de li Tappi.

A little later, on my left, I came upon the first of many wayside shrines, a doghouse-sized structure, dark brown on the base, ochre on the upper section. A small arched opening was covered by a rusted wire grating, kept secure with an equally rusted padlock. Further along was another shrine, that one dedicated to Our Lady of Sorrows. I wondered whether that might be an omen for what lay ahead. Soon enough I would come to think so, today's bright sun and dry footpath giving way, on all too many days, to driving rain and mud. Shrines such as these are everywhere in rural Italy. Many are decrepit, those who once cared for them having died, younger generations no longer being interested in what the shrines meant or why they were erected in the first place. Looking at these melancholy testaments to lost devotion, I was reminded of something written more than a century earlier on the other side of the Alps.

Jacques Rivière to Paul Claudel: "I see that Christianity is dying... We no longer know what those spires are doing above our towns since they are no longer the prayer of any of us. We do not know the meaning of those great buildings, surrounded today by railroad stations and hospitals, and from which the people themselves have chased the monks. We do not know what those stucco crosses stand for on graves, encrusted, moreover, with a revolting art." Rivière was 21 when he wrote this in 1907. Claudel was 39. Rivière would become a man of letters. Claudel already was one and would be much more: poet, dramatist, diplomat (among other postings, from 1928 to 1933 he was France's ambassador to the United States). Each was a convert—more particularly, a returnee. Each would have understood what I felt as I contemplated the wayside shrines.

I headed slightly uphill, first southwest, then turned abruptly north toward Oricchio and its four dozen buildings, a quarter of them vacant and more than thirty of them a century or more old. The Cammino arrived at the entrance to Oricchio but immediately hairpinned to the west, toward Fogliano, a relative metropolis with 120 residents.

I came to a fallow field that gleamed white in the midday sun. The ground was equal parts dirt and stones; if anything, the stones predominated. It was reminiscent of the coastal sections of Croatia—the island of Lošinj in particular—where farmers had to invent their fields by laboriously removing stones much larger than these, stones so large that the result was high stone walls surrounding small plots of still-stony but now plantable soil. I suppose the residual stones, there as well as in Italy, might have beneficial effects. They might keep parched soil from turning into the Mediterranean equivalent of Death Valley's dry playas. The stones might prevent the soil from becoming impervious to crops' roots.

Elsewhere, for most of my walk, the fields had been green, so green as to be almost oppressive. I'm not used to green, a color infrequently found in the American Southwest, particularly at low elevations, and, when found, invariably surrounded by vari-colored soil and the blue-gray of granite or the rust-brown of sandstone. Here green was ubiquitous, except where fields were left fallow. Along the roadway, in this section and in the whole stretch from Norcia, the fields were uniformly green. I couldn't identify most of the crops. This was May, and the plants were not mature; they looked indistinguishable except for their height.

Immediately adjacent to the roadway, and later along the paths once the roadway had given way to narrower routes, were flowers. The first few feet alongside the Cammino hadn't been turned over by tractors, hadn't had pesticides applied to them, and there plants ran riot. I came across flowers I never could see at home. After passing that stony field the grass was punctuated by green-winged orchids, standing proudly tall in their purple finery, their stalks like asparagus spears, their blooms making me wonder why they are called green-winged instead of purple-winged. Further on I came across equally purple but less attractive specimens of *orchis purpurea Hudson*, which rose from the ground on dark stalks. My wife cultivates orchids, no species of which is native to Southern California, but in the lower elevations of the Apennines orchids were as plentiful as my native place's yuccas.

After Oricchio the path was more woodsy, and in a kilometer I came upon another water trough—actually, a series of two concrete troughs more than a foot deep. At one end a faucet poured a constant stream into the first trough, which was six inches higher than the second trough. Water from the first spilled into the second, and from the second it spilled onto the ground, disappearing downhill. On each trough floated a thick bed of algae. What self-respecting horse would drink here? Of what other use were the troughs? I had no answer for either question.

As I entered Fogliano I came to a farmhouse, or what I took to be a farmhouse, that sported two long rows of solar panels adjacent to the road, which at least temporarily had returned to asphalt. There were forty large panels. Facing them across the road was a low stone wall on which large, faded letters greeted passersby: "Buongiorno!" Most of the houses in Fogliano were of twentieth-century construction. Given the recurrence of seismic activity in the region, I was surprised to see how many of the newer homes were built of bricks. In Southern California, which has a lower incidence of earthquakes than does this part of Italy, bricks are not building materials but only decorative materials. Perhaps the bricks here were reinforced, but still. One good shudder and cracks would appear, even if a structure were in no danger of collapse.

Just beyond Fogliano I passed fields of young hay, and the forward prospect was one reminiscent of the rolling hills of home, but with low green bushes substituted for low gray scrub. Cypresses paraded in a level field to my right, while the sloped field to my left was devoid of any plant taller than a foot. Following the guidebook, I next found myself on an overgrown dirt road, trees and bushes now thick on either side, the median green with grass. To the right and left, peeking out at me, were flowers I never had seen before, some clearly in the orchid family but others reminiscent of daisies and sunflowers and angel's breath.

I went around a bend and was greeted with growls and barks. I paused, thinking I might be confronted by angry canines, but no dogs approached me. Proceeding cautiously, I came to a chicken-wire enclosure behind which I could see several dog houses and several dogs, each a different breed. Some put their snouts into the chicken wire and conveyed their greetings; others merely stared. I supposed not many people passed by, so the sight of a hiker might have been a pleasant diversion for the dogs. The undergrowth was so thick behind their enclosure that I could see no outbuilding or house, but people must have lived nearby.

Leaving the dogs, after politely returning their greetings, I came across isolated poppies. I had been seeing them since around Popoli—larger than the poppies of California and red instead of golden. These were the poppies of John McCrae's Flanders fields and were, appropriately, the color of blood. Back home, in the Golden State, I was familiar only with yellow poppies, a happier color but not contrasting as well as the red with the deep green that was everywhere around me along the Cammino.

Earlier in the year, after Southern California had experienced an uncommonly wet rainy season, wildflowers bloomed with delightful vigor. Whole hillsides were carpeted in white, blue, or yellow—sometimes all three colors together. Near Lake Elsinore poppies were in extravagance. So remarkable was the display that tens of thousands of gawkers came from Los Angeles and San Diego, bringing traffic to a halt for miles in every direction. Not content to view the display from roadside, many people walked into the acres of poppies, perhaps imagining themselves in the scene from *The Wizard of Oz* in which Dorothy and her companions danced through a field of poppies growing so thickly that thousands of blooms must have met their demise for the sake of cinematographic delight.

Soon I was back on a paved road and moved speedily. The road was straight for hundreds of feet at a time. A Fiat passed me, and I realized how few vehicles I had seen since leaving Norcia—five or six cars, no doubt driven by locals (who else would be on these isolated roads?), and one or two pieces of farm machinery but no trucks and no pickups (do such even exist in Italy?). I came to a rare signpost. It said Norcia was 13.5 kilometers behind me, Cascia four kilometers ahead. It was comforting to have confirmation that I had not spent the day walking in the wrong direction.

I was on Strada Provinciale 474 and came to a junction. A signpost told me that Cascia was now only 3.5 kilometers ahead. I did quick mental calculations. How many minutes had it taken to cover the half kilometer? How many miles per hour did that equate to? My goal was to walk at two and a half miles per hour along good roads, a rate comparable to what I was used to at home. Given that I carried a pack, I would settle for two miles per hour. I exceeded that between the two signposts, and that gave me a sense of satisfaction.

For a while the road was two lanes, though there was no center stripe to mark them off. I had not seen a sidewalk since leaving Norcia. Here, as the road began a long, winding downhill, I would have welcomed a sidewalk. I had to walk on the roadway. I didn't know the Italian custom, but I walked facing traffic, to give myself a slightly better chance to dodge dodgy vehicles. Sometimes there was no place to dodge to, the side of the road being a cliff, either upward or downward. Fortunately traffic remained sparse, and the day was so quiet that I could hear an approaching vehicle well in advance.

More worrisome than the prospect of being struck was the certainty of losing the elevation I had gained since leaving Piediripa. The incline had been almost imperceptible through Fogliano, but now elevation was lost rapidly. I could see the valley into which I would descend, only to climb out of it again to reach the heights of Cascia. I was reminded that, throughout my hikes in California's Sierra Nevada, on trails that gain and lose hundreds or even thousands of feet with discouraging regularity, I have searched in vain for the El Dorado of trails, one designed by the artist M. C. Escher: a trail that is downhill in both directions. I have yet to stumble across it either in the Sierra Nevada or the Apennines.

I reached Padule, a *frazione* (Americans might say neighborhood or community) of Cascia. It marked the low point, topographically though not metaphorically. I would see multiple low points of the latter sort later on in my journey, but after Padule the rest of the afternoon was uphill. I passed through an industrial area, turned sharply right up a dirt road, gained and then lost elevation, took a shortcut along a street closed to traffic, and ended up at a roundabout. From there it was a steady slog toward Cascia, built, like most Italian towns, on a hill for reasons of fortification. By this time I was tired and in no mood to admire what towered above me. I could make out the basilica dedicated to St. Rita, she and it the pride of Cascia, but my only interest at the moment was in reaching the hotel where a reservation awaited me. I had not come especially far, only eighteen kilometers, but I was ready for a nap and for food more substantial than the snacks I carried.

Hotel delle Rose was across the street from the basilica. I knew that if I made a beeline for the latter's cupola, I would find my lodging. So it was up Via Lucentini, then up Via IV Novembre and up Via Leonina Porta, and finally, in a circuitous and inefficient way, up Via Santa Chiara and Via Fasce to the entrance to the hotel, which may or may not have been the nicest in Cascia but certainly was the closest to the basilica, a chief goal of St. Rita's many pilgrims. Check-in was perfunctory. I had a longer conversation with the dogs than with the desk clerk. From my room I looked over a wide valley that ended in low hills backed by taller hills. Houses below me were cream, white, or yellow, none newly painted. Their roofs were tessellated with brown, gray, or dappled tiles. The lovely effect was marred by rooftop solar panels that proved I was not looking down on a nineteenth-century scene.

I took an evening constitutional. First I visited the basilica, which faced away from the hotel. I walked up a side street and circled into the nave. A few people were coming and going, praying or touring. In a side chapel, under a golden canopy, was a glass case containing St. Rita's body. Women knelt at a rail that prevented anyone getting close to the reliquary. I couldn't tell if that was Rita's actual face I saw or a mask. I presumed the latter. I took a few steps back, to make room for others, and looked one by one at the kneeling women. With St. Jude, St. Rita is known as the saint for impossible causes. What insoluble things were these women asking her intercession on? Had she intervened on their behalf once, and were they now asking further help? Had they been asking for years, with as yet no evident reply?

I went outside. Before me were two arcades, one on either side of a road that stretched straight for a long block. Half way down, on the left, was the tourist information bureau, but it was closed. Beyond it was a switchbacked staircase leading to a narrow, precipitous, stepped alley that dropped past several houses and disgorged walkers on a parallel road far below. During my December trip I descended the staircase and began to descend the alley but thought the better of it, since its steps were iced over. This time I went to the bottom, turned right, and explored what was along the lower road. At the end was the Convent of St. Augustine. Before it was the road from the front of the basilica. I retraced my steps, went past the alley I had descended, and took the lower road two more blocks to Via Fasce, which I ascended to the hotel. The medieval quarter of Cascia I found less interesting than the apparently older medieval quarters of two towns I later visited, Guarcino and Castel di Tora. Perhaps it was the relative bustle of Cascia. Neither Guarcino nor Castel di Tora boasts a saint of Rita's prominence. At neither do buses unload hundreds of pilgrims each day. Cascia has kept the medieval form, but I sensed that Guarcino and Castel di Tora have kept more of the medieval spirit. More on them later.

The Saint of Lost Causes

As IS MY unfortunate custom, I woke early. Although it was May, at that hour the sky was more dark than light, the sun itself being not quite awake. I went through the morning ritual: shave, shower, dress, wonder—wondering what I had forgotten to bring, wondering what I already had misplaced, wondering what my plan for the day was.

I knew the first part of my plan: breakfast. Weeks before, while planning this walk, I thought how convenient it was going to be to lose weight as a matter of course. How could you not lose weight, when walking 305 kilometers in up-and-down terrain? How could you not lose weight, when there would be no fast-food temptations along the way, when you'd have to carry your lunch and snacks (extra weight!) and so would minimize them, when you'd be unsure how to interpret what the trattoria or hotel menu offered in the evening and so you'd select sparingly, leaving the table not quite full?

Not that I was fat, but I had some fat I wanted to lose. A drop of ten pounds would be a happy reward when getting home, but it was not to be, except fleetingly. I did get home a few pounds lighter, but those pounds returned in a few days. Probably they had been stowaways in my luggage, just waiting to return to American soil. I couldn't blame their subterfuge for seeing no change on the scale. I had to blame myself.

At home I eat the sparest of breakfasts, often just a cup of tea. Sometimes tea plus toast, lightly covered with margarine and strawberry jam. One might think that with breakfasts like these I'd be on a perpetual slow weight loss, but not so. My morning half-fast invariably is canceled out by late afternoon, after a normal lunch and a snack (except when I'm able to discipline myself during Lent).

Such has been my breakfast routine for years. My weight has held steady, but it's been ten pounds above what I'd be satisfied with and higher still above what I once read would be my ideal weight, based on my height and general body build. Decades ago I came across a chart that said a man of my height and build should weigh between 175 and 180 pounds. Giving complete credence to what I read (and why not?), I made 177.5 pounds my long-range goal. I once reached that weight, after strenuous workouts and faithful attention to diet, but I reached it for exactly one day and then, like a comet after reaching its perigee, I moved away to what by then had become my usual weight.

There are three body types for men: mesomorph, endomorph, and ectomorph.

Mesomorphs have standard proportions, with regular musculature and no obvious excess fat, at least in their younger years. In school these were the good athletes. Usually they were the worst students, so that was some compensation for the rest of us.

Endomorphs are heavy-set and tend toward fat. They claim

their extra poundage comes from having big bones, but that's not really it. A 200-pound man of normal proportions is said to have about 30 pounds of bones. A "big-boned" man weighing 240 pounds might have 35 pounds of bones, hardly enough to account for the weight difference. The rest is blubber, something endomorphs are prone to.

Me? I always was an ectomorph—tall and thin. Ectomorphs have less musculature than mesomorphs (just as many muscles, of course, but the muscles are smaller and less defined). As kids, ectomorphs are skinny. That's how I was. When I was in high school, my mother made me four peanut butter and jelly sand- wiches for lunch. They tided me over until I got home, when I made myself two more, to get myself to dinner. The peanut butter was Skippy's smooth, and the jelly was Welch's grape. The bread was Wonder Bread. (Only years later did I figure out why it was called that: because it was a wonder that it qualified as bread at all.)

That was my routine until I went away to college, at which point I largely gave up sandwiches. By the time I was in the depths of middle age, I had settled into my current routine of tea alone or tea with toast for breakfast, but the toast isn't Wonder Bread (usually it's Japanese *shokupan*), and the grape jelly trans- mogrified into strawberry jam. Instead of twelve slices of bread per day (the six sandwiches of yesteryear), I limit myself to one or two. Any more than that and I gain weight. I've managed to maintain a plateau for years, but it's a plateau I want to descend from by ten pounds, and I thought walking through Italy would accomplish that.

It didn't, because every place I stayed offered free breakfasts. I wasn't about to let free food escape me when I had paid dearly for my accommodations—and even when I had paid modestly, which usually was the case. When I went downstairs to Hotel delle Rose's breakfast room, I delighted in the offerings. I didn't know that later in my journey I would tire of seeing the same offerings everywhere. There were fruit, cheese, cereal, prosciutto, juice, coffee, tea, and the inescapable toast. I let little go unsampled. After all, I had a long day of hiking in front of me, and the more I packed in now, the less snacking I would need to do along the way—indisputably logical but not conducive to weight loss.

Back in my room from breakfast, I looked carefully in every corner. Had I left something behind? I expected to. It's easy to overlook something in plain sight. I looked in the small places, and then I stepped back and looked in the large places. I stood at the door and took a wide view of the room. I patted my pockets. Phone, wallet, passport. They were all there. With them I could go anywhere. Without them I could go nowhere. Perhaps I worried too much about leaving something behind, but if I found myself unpacking at tonight's stop and realized that I had left something crucial behind, I might have no way to retrieve it but to retrace my steps, no public transportation being available.

As I say, it's easy in a hotel room to overlook something, so I always double and triple check. My insistence on doing so may have developed from my years as a magazine editor. I remember working diligently on an article about the nature of God. The title was "God Has No Body." I adjusted the title more than once before settling on this wording. I proofread the body text repeatedly, finding a few typos and then, on the last pass, finding none. This article and all the others seemed fine, and off the magazine went to the printer.

It came back with this article titled "God Has No Bobody." I had focused so much on catching the smallest error in the body copy that I was blind to an inch-tall typo in the title. I waited for an onslaught of carping messages from readers. "How could you make such a blunder?" I heard nothing. It couldn't have been that no one noticed. It must have been that they thought the title appeared as I had intended it, that I was being clever. I wondered whether they thought I had in mind Shirley Ellis's 1964 song "The Name Game," an early verse being this:

> Lincoln! Lincoln, Lincoln. bo-bin-coln
> Bo-na-na fanna, fo-fin-coln
> Fee fi mo-min-coln, Lincoln!

Maybe readers thought I wanted them to think:

> Body! Body, body, bo-body
> Bo-na-na fanna, fo-fo-dy
> Fee fi mo-mo-dy, body!

I figured I lucked out. My oversight didn't result in endless ribbing, but an oversight on a pilgrimage might not have as happy a consequence, so I checked and rechecked.

Out of Hotel delle Rose, I took a last look at St. Rita's basilica, turned left down a steep grade, then left again and left again, onto a road that lay behind the hotel. In two minutes I came to a blockage. Across the road, stretching from a vertical cliff on the left to a sheer falloff on the right, were laid several K-rails. That's how they're designated in California, but most of the U.S. knows them as Jersey barriers. For reasons unknown to me the authorities wanted no cars to travel further along this road. Perhaps they wanted no hikers to pass either, since there was no opening left for anyone on foot to squeeze through. I knew the footpath I needed to take was ahead on the left, so, with my pack encumbering me, I crawled over the barricade and continued downhill.

At a curve in the road I found a steep, stepped path marked St. Rita's Way. Halfway up the cliffside the path leveled out. It was narrow and covered deeply in duff. Corroded pipe fencing was on the downhill side, at least where the drop was precipitous. Thin trees on either side sent tendrils across the path. I had to look downward so as not to stumble across rocks hidden by fallen leaves and forward so as not to be whipped in the face by thin branches. At one point the path was squeezed between a drop-off and overhanging granite. The metal fence there leaned outward, as though shying away from the blue-gray mass threatening to roll over it.

Further on I found a tree fallen across the path. It, like all the trees, was thin—no redwoods here—and I managed to squeeze through the triangle it formed between cliff and drop-off. Then I realized that this trail had not been maintained recently. Days later I would read that the K-rails had been put in place because recent storms had caused severe erosion all along the escarpment from which the trail hung. If there was danger of rock collapsing onto the road below, there was greater danger of the trail I was on falling apart. At the time I was oblivious of this—and just as well.

The day before, as I walked from Norcia to Cascia, I marveled at the bright green of the fields and hills. Here I was in the midst of the green. It was lovely (later during my hike I would find it occasionally suffocating), but there was so much foliage that views were blocked. I could see a distance only when the trail was straight and even then only along the trail corridor itself. The only sign of life I saw on St. Rita's Way, other than bushes and trees, was a snail with a white shell. I never before had come across one like that.

At length the trail descended to the level of the road I had left after the K-rails, and it came to a signboard that stood next to a wooden bridge. The bridge was of modern construction but deeply weathered. Under it ran a stream, and at the far end was the main road. A right turn would lead back to Cascia, a left turn to Roccaporena, the hamlet where St. Rita had lived. On the near end of the bridge's handrail was a Cammino di San Benedetto marker with a white arrow telling me to cross to the road. I dutifully complied. At the other end I removed my pack and rested. The air was neither warm nor cool, and I had been moving leisurely enough not to build up a sweat. The leafy trail, for all its disarray, had been pleasant. Now I faced a long road-side walk.

The pavement snaked through a narrow valley. At one point it was squeezed between the stream on my left and a twenty-meter cliff on my right. The cliff was of fractious stone, and to protect vehicles and walkers from falling debris there was another of those half-tunnels: solid concrete against the cliff and as a roof but eight widely-spaced pillars on the stream side. And no side-walk or shoulder within the overhang. I walked against traffic, hoping there would be none. A driver rounding the bend leading into the overhang would have only a few seconds to spot me in the shadows—a discomfiting thought. (Headline: "American Hiker Flattened in Apennine Tunnel.")

It wasn't long before I spotted in the distance a building high on a stalagmitic outcropping; it was the Sacro Scoglio, dedicated to St. Rita and located above Roccaporena. To reach the top pilgrims follow the Via Crucis up three hundred steps. This is where the saint used to go to pray, and it is said that she prayed so long that her knees and elbows left impressions in the rocks.

She was born Margherita Lotti in Roccaporena in 1381. Although Rita, as she was known, wanted to dedicated her life to God, her parents forced her to marry Paolo Mancini, who, as an officer, had a higher rank than most townsfolk. He was an obdurate man. She put up with him and saw to the upbringing of their twin boys. When the boys were yet far from adulthood, their father was murdered, a consequence of political infighting, and they vowed revenge on the killers, whom Rita immediately had forgiven. When she learned of their intention, she prayed that they might be prevented from committing a crime in return. That came to pass, but at great distress to Rita. Both boys fell ill and died.

Now free, however sadly, to enter the religious life, Rita sought entrance at the Augustinian establishment in Cascia. She repeatedly was refused by the abbess, who feared Rita's presence within the walls might bring a blood feud into the monastery. But one morning, despite the doors having been locked the night before, the abbess discovered Rita inside, and she realized it was God's will that Rita enter the religious life. (It was said that she had been transported over the walls by her patrons, Sts. Augustine, John the Baptist, and Nicholas of Tolentino.)

The abbess, still unsure of Rita, gave her a test. She ordered her to water a dead plant. The newcomer obeyed, and the plant returned to life. It is said that a vine that now stands in the cloister was that plant, but if so it might be the world's oldest vine. However that may be, what seems indisputable is that for the last fifteen years of her life Rita had what is called "the gift of the thorn," a painful stigmata on her forehead. She had spent much time praying before images of a thorn-crowned Christ, and her wish to share in his sufferings seems to have been granted in a distinctive manner.

Rita remained part of the monastery, dying in May 1457. (She was canonized in 1900.) The previous winter she prayed to know whether her prayers of atonement for her violent husband and sons had borne fruit on their behalf. Her answer came in the monastery's snow-covered garden, where a rose bloomed and two figs ripened, the rose representing her husband, the figs her sons. She came to be known as the saint of desperate or lost causes.

As I approached Roccaporena I saw, high on a hillside to my right, a large natural cave. In it stood a tall cross. A path led up to it, but I declined to ascend. I equally declined to climb to the even higher Sacro Scoglio. Although I had come only five kilometers from Cascia, I felt my energy draining. Jet lag finally seemed to be kicking in. I still had nine kilometers to go to reach my lodgings, and most of the way would be uphill.

I walked into Roccaporena, passing the Casa Maritale, the house where Rita and her husband had lived and where their sons had been born. I looked through the gated doorway of the small structure. At the far end of the main room—now a chapel—was an altar with a large, seventeenth-century painting behind it. The painting, by Luca Giordano, depicted a kneeling Rita praying before a Crucifix, with a pair of chubby putti floating above her. One of them held a wreath of roses and appeared ready to drop it squarely on her head. The painting was fine, but it would have been finer without the putti.

At the far end of the hamlet, below street level, was a church, the Santuario di Santa Rita, constructed after World War II to accommodate the increasing number of pilgrims devoted to the saint. In earlier times Roccaporena had few visitors because of the difficulty of reaching the place, first along dirt paths and then along a dirt road. Now tour buses come on an asphalt road, disgorging their occupants in a large lot at the far end of town.

Ten feet below street level, I sat on the wall of the fountain in front of the Santuario and fretted. I had no great interest in St. Rita—her appeal is chiefly to motherly types—and Roccaporena seemed crowded, even though objectively it was not. Since leaving Cascia I had been alone. I had seen no one on the cliffside trail (understandably, because they likely had been aware that St. Rita's Way was closed, while I had been unaware of the closure), and I had been passed by only a few cars while walking along the road between the footbridge at the end of the trail and Roccaporena. I had had time for my thoughts and the quiet to entertain them. Roccaporena wasn't quiet, though compared to Rome it would have been called somnambulant. Still, I itched to move on, to leave the day-trippers and the idle chatter.

I gathered up my things, putting away the remains of a snack I had fished out of my pack, and returned to the roadbed, turning left toward the far end of town, which was only a few hundred steps away. Beyond the bus lot the road curved right and then made a hairpin left turn, climbing steeply. A five-minute walk put me high above the town, which looked all the finer from a distance. After a kilometer and a half I came to a sign marking an even smaller village, Capanne di Roccaporena. Opposite the sign a trail left the road, and soon I again was alone.

The trail passed through wooded land, climbing slowly

higher, passing on the right Monte Roccaporena (1,149 m.) and then Monte Femasino (1,171 m.), the high points along the day's route. The path leveled out, and my arms swung freely as I made good speed, a trekking pole in each hand. Nearing a ridge line, I passed a meadow in bloom. It was covered thickly in grasses, some hugging the ground, others stretching toward the sun. In the center of the meadow was a large patch of small lavender flowers. They were most abundant at the meadow's low point; perhaps only the grasses there had received enough water to justify displaying their glory. Later, as the sky became clouded, I glimpsed a distant farmstead through a stand of skinny trees that had not yet returned to full foliage. The field next to the farmhouse was smoothly green, but what was the crop? It was too far away to tell.

My knowledge of plant life is minimal. City- and sub-urb-bred, I never had a chance to live in the countryside and never was diligent enough to study guidebooks from which I could learn to distinguish crops, flowers, and trees. I recognize some but not many. Most of my outdoor time is spent hiking in California and Arizona, in the Sierra Nevada and Grand Canyon. The latter is largely devoid of botanical interest—a few species of cacti, scrub, mesquite, and almost nothing that blooms—but the mountains of central California feature plants so various that over the years I purchased several books listing and identifying what I might see along the trails, but for the most part those books have remained unread, another example of intentions not realized in actions.

I walked on, passing makeshift fencing: a field bounded by two strands of barbed wire stretched between posts that more properly should be called sticks—and rickety ones at that. The fencing seemed insufficient to keep cattle in and trespassers out. Who, of the few people using the path, would have wanted to go into the field, which, from the height of the overgrowth, seemed not to have been tilled in decades? Had there been a time, years ago, when hikers, caught by the late hour or bad weather, departed from the trail and set up camp in the field, only to leave it littered and the owner cursing backpackers?

A Chariot and Wise Admonitions

BEFORE LEAVING CASCIA I had intended to go the full eighteen kilometers from that town to Monteleone di Spoleto, as recommended in the guidebook, but, when I called ahead on the day I left Cascia, the few lodging places in Monteleone were full. I should have phoned a day earlier, as I left Norcia. The only place I could find with a vacancy was the Agriturismo di Colle del Capitano, which was at the fourteen-kilometer mark from Cascia. It turned out to be a *felix culpa*.

I neared the agriturismo in the middle of the afternoon. The path opened up and became a road, and from a height I looked down on my soon-to-be lodgings. I worried that I was early, too early to check in by Italian standards, so I walked slowly, stopping often, looking at the small valley.

Down there, in 1902, a sixth-century B.C. Etruscan chariot was unearthed. The chariot is made chiefly of bronze, with some wood and ivory, and has sculpted representations of Achilles, Memnon, and other figures. It is a parade chariot, not a war chariot, and it is said to be the best-preserved of the world's three hundred extant ancient chariots. It accommodated two, the driver and his honored guest. This chariot was used in a tomb burial, somewhat as pharaohs were entombed in their pyramids along with their finest possessions.

The chariot was discovered when a farmer and his son were constructing a house. (Was it the two-story building I saw below?) They sold it to a scrap dealer who, blessedly, didn't scrap it. The chariot didn't remain in the area long. The year after its discovery it was purchased by New York's Metropolitan Museum of Art, where it still resides.

The purchase was effected by Luigi Parma di Cesnola, an Italian-American who was the director of the museum, a position he held from 1879 until his death in 1904. He had seen military service in the Sardinian, British, and American armies, having fought in the First Italian War of Independence, the Crimean War, and the American Civil War.

An amateur archaeologist, he served as an American consul in Cyprus. His official duties likely weren't burdensome, since he had enough free time to dig up 35,000 antiquities. Most of them made it to New York, but 5,000 were lost at sea when the ship carrying them sank. The remaining 30,000 pieces were purchased from Palma di Cesnola by the newly-enlarged museum in 1872. That may have had something to do with his becoming the museum's director seven years later.

I couldn't help but wonder what that scrap dealer ultimately thought of what had been so briefly in his hands, and I wondered all the more how the farmer and his son could have seen so little value in the chariot that they sold it for scrap.

The road I was on was straight and descended the shoulder of the hill on the right side of the valley. In the distance I saw the low point, with the road continuing straight ahead and disappearing behind foliage and with a turnoff to the left that led to the agriturismo. Turning there, I spotted a sign that assured me I was in the right place. At the far end was what I took to be the main house. It was the two-story building I had seen from higher up. It had no prominent signage. On my right I passed a much newer building that proved to be four guest rooms. On the left was an older but not old building; more lodging space, I thought. Beyond the main house, to its left, was a fourth building. I would discover later what it was.

I rang the bell. The door was opened by Piera, a delightful woman of later middle age. She welcomed me in, instructed me to set down my backpack, and pointed to a seat at one of the tables against the right wall. Time for food, she said. She excused herself to the open kitchen, which was just beyond, and I heard the clatter of cutlery and the piling up of platters. Out came bread, wine, salad, spaghetti, and sausages made on the farm. There were sliced meats, stewed meats, sweets, cheese, and bruschetta.

The door I had entered opened and in came Saverio, Piera's son, with containers of goat milk. He said the farm had fifty goats in addition to cows. I asked about other animals. I had seen half a dozen dogs as I approached, each a different breed. Saverio said their main job was to keep wild boars and other intruders off the property. He said the agriturismo also had horses and that he rode frequently. He eyed his mother, who said that she no longer rode horses, only bikes.

After lunch I was shown to my room. It was in the first building I had come to. It was spacious not just by European standards but by American standards. I settled in, opened the shutters, and briefly watched the dogs—the small ones scampering, the large ones lying quietly. I took a cue from the latter, slipped off my shoes, and reclined on the bed. I had expected more rustication at an agriturismo and was content not to have found it. I had stayed at an agriturismo only once before, and its accommodations had lived up to my low expectations. This room was as joyous as the proprietors.

Freshened up, I later returned to the main house for dinner. I was the lone diner but not the lone entrant. As I sat before my plate, the door repeatedly opened. Young people well known to Piera came in, greeted her with kisses, and exited carrying platters of food, mostly meat but vegetables too. The scene was repeated several times. Saverio had told me that the farm sold its goods in Leonessa and elsewhere—even in Rome, as I recall—so I thought that these may have been locals coming by for their weekly supply, but it was strange that they should walk out with uncovered platters rather than with sealed boxes.

I struggled to finish the food. Most of what I was served was familiar to me; a few things I had to ask about. All of it was good, but there was too much *all*. I had been given a large lunch only a few hours before, and dinner wasn't notably smaller. I said good night and returned to my room. If I had lost any weight on the day's hike, the loss was more than canceled out by Piera's culinary skills.

Wanting to get an early start the next day, I got into bed early but had trouble falling asleep. People kept passing under my window, talking loudly. Sometimes they stopped under the window and talked loudly. Cars kept coming and going. I could hear their doors slamming and people laughing. I opened the shutters slightly and looked toward the building behind the main house. That's where people were headed, and for the next six hours that's where the main noise came from. The noise didn't abate until the end of what turned out to be a lengthy wedding reception, the last revelers driving away at 3:15 a.m. Perhaps it took that long to finish off the platters. I finally was able to drop off to sleep, knowing my intention to depart early would be unfulfilled.

I woke to stiff rain. Looking out, I saw no dogs and only one or two cars. Skipping around puddles, I made my way to the main house, where Piera was as perky as she had been the night before. Breakfast was sufficient but thankfully small. I was spared the guilt of having to leave something on my plate. As I ate, I listened to the rain and dreaded what lay ahead of me. My dread was dispelled quickly, when Saverio offered to drive me to Leonessa, where I had a reservation at the Leo Hotel. A pilgrimage purist would have insisted on walking through the downpour, but I feared catching cold more than I feared not maintaining a reputation as an intrepid hiker.

Before we reached the hotel Saverio gave me a bit of a tour of Leonessa. The forecast was for equally foul weather the next day, and I expected that prudence would force me to take the next leg, to Rieti, by bus. Saverio showed me the bus stop, pointing out where I should wait and checking the timetable. It turned out not to be a long walk from the hotel, where he dropped me off and wished me a "Buon Cammino!"

The Leo Hotel seemed preposterously large for Leonessa, a town of 2,700. The hotel wasn't the only lodging in town, yet it had eighty rooms. As it turned out, only two or three were occupied. When I walked in the door, I found a grumpy clerk behind the counter. He gave me my key and pointed down a hallway that led to the elevator to my room, which turned out to be adequate but not up to the previous night's standards. It was a handicap room with an absurdly high toilet. I'm long-legged, but even my legs couldn't reach the floor. I wondered how a short Italian grandmother could have managed her latrinal exercises.

After unpacking, I headed downstairs and found the clerk at the other end of the lobby, watching television. I asked him a question about a location on my map, and from then on he was voluble and pleasant. The rain having stopped, I headed out to check dining establishments, the hotel not having any. I used Google Maps, going several blocks in one direction to find a pizzeria that only provided take-out service, then several blocks in another direction to find a restaurant that was closed for the day. The pickings were slim. I ended up at a restaurant where diners were few (it was early) and the waiter officious. He stood near my table, watching the door for patrons who, he must have known, wouldn't come until later in the evening.

I finished my meal while it still was light and decided an evening constitutional was in order. I walked down a narrow street where I found an archway covering a trough fountain. A slow stream of water fell from a protruding stone outlet into the center of a ten-foot-long basin. The outlet was too close to the water's top for a bottle to be held under it, so I wondered whether the fountain had been intended for watering horses rather than for providing drinking water for residents.

I crossed into another street, Via di San Francesco, and came upon a stone church. It was dedicated to a local St. Francis, not the one from Assisi, and was wrapped in nine wide ratchet bands that were stretched horizontally across the façade from eye level to the roof line. The bands were taut around the sides of the building and were attached to concrete anchors embedded in the ground halfway to the rear. On the façade the bands pressed against eight wooden slats that ran the whole vertical distance, but at the corners the slats were replaced by right-angle brackets made of steel, the better to hold the stonework in place. The earthquakes that had leveled much of Norcia had reached Leonessa too.

Across the road that fronted the church was Piazza Garibaldi (every Italian town seems to have a Piazza Garibaldi) with a small fountain in the center, several potted plants, and a few benches. I crossed the piazza, passed into a *vicolo* so narrow that no sumo wrestler could have traversed it, and turned left onto Via delle Mole. In a few moments I came to the Santuario di San Giuseppe da Leonessa, the town's patron saint. This church had an open but gated door. I was unable to enter but could peer inside. At the far end metal scaffolding rose into the dome. Through the scaffolding I could see an illuminated, glass-fronted reliquary above and behind the freestanding altar. The reliquary was too far away for me to see it clearly, but it appeared to contain the saint's body—or at least some saint's body.

San Giuseppe was born in 1556 into a family of wealthy wool merchants. His birth name was Eufranio Desideri. After he was orphaned his uncle, under whose care he was placed, sent him to Viterbo for his education. He later returned to Leonessa and then went to Spoleto, where he joined the Capuchin order, an offshoot of the Franciscans that had been created two generations earlier.

Ordained in 1580, Giuseppe undertook an active rather than cloistered life. He traveled to Istanbul to comfort enslaved Christians, having studied the Turkish language and culture. He procured an audience with Sultan Murad III, from whom he requested religious freedom for those converting to Christianity or returning to it. The Sultan does not seem to have been pleased. Giuseppe was sentence to death but somehow managed to return to Italy (some say that, like St. Peter, he was released from his shackles by an angel). He wandered throughout Italy, preaching to the poor and, among other charitable works, establishing a grain bank that loaned seeds to destitute farmers. To Giuseppe are attributed not just the reconciliation of irreconcilable families but healings and even the multiplication of loaves and beans (no, not fishes). He died in 1612 and was canonized in 1746. His feast day is February 4, which just happens to be my wife's birthday.

Back in my room, I thought about the man in whose steps, at least approximately, I was walking.

"Idleness is the enemy of the soul." Those are the opening words of chapter forty-eight of St. Benedict's Rule, the chapter in which he counsels daily manual labor. The Benedictine Order's motto is *Ora et Labora*, "Pray and Work." Monks should do both, said Benedict. I rarely have done enough of either.

When I first read the saint's admonition, I thought of a comparable one written in 1779 by Samuel Johnson to his future biographer, James Boswell: "If you are idle, be not solitary; if you are solitary, be not idle." Johnson was extending for Boswell's benefit a precept given by Robert Burton in *The Anatomy of Melancholy* more than a century earlier: "Be not solitary, be not idle." Johnson told Boswell that Burton's "great direction" was left "to men disordered like you." For all his virtues, Boswell indeed led a disordered life. Johnson cherished him nevertheless, delighting in his company while reproving his faults, most of which Boswell acknowledged even publicly.

I have all of Johnson's writings, some in multiple scholarly editions, and many of the writings referring to him by his contemporaries. Burton clearly was an important influence on the young Johnson, and Johnson has been an important influence on the not-so-young me. I have tried to learn from him. One of the reasons I have been attracted to Johnson is that I share some of his defects and foibles, dilatoriness being perhaps the most besetting. I am a master at putting things off, perhaps the one area in which I excel Johnson, who often castigated himself for procrastination. In his private reflections, which have been preserved for us in his diaries and annals, Johnson faulted himself repeatedly for wasting time and not getting much done, yet the Yale Edition of his collected works goes to twenty-one large volumes. I compare my own meager output—meager both in length and in quality—and I recognize that I have had much more justification for self-recrimination than did Johnson.

Procrastination was not something Benedict allowed his monks. There would be no shortcuts. In chapter eighteen of the Rule he said that monks who sing fewer than the entire 150 psalms in the course of a week "show themselves lazy in the service of devotion." To shame them, he contrasted what they were called to do with what the earliest Fathers of the Church were said to have done. Those holy men prayed the entire psalter in a single day. How little, Benedict said, he was asking of the men under him!

He was keen to have his monks lead balanced lives—lives balanced between the cares of the world (work) and the cares of eternity (prayer). He gave them in his Rule a schematic for doing that, and his schematic might be the most successful ever laid out. It certainly has been the longest-lived, still in use today, with hardly an adjustment, after a millennium and a half.

Benedict composed the Rule near the end of his religious career. It was not something that could have been written by a man inexperienced in the requirements of the monastic life. After his formative years at Subiaco he moved south, to Montecassino, which lies about 150 kilometers to the southeast of Rome. On a mountaintop site that had featured a temple to Apollo he founded an abbey and served as its first abbot. There he composed the Rule.

Of course the abbey of his time bore no resemblance to the abbey of recent times. Today's Montecassino—faithfully reconstructed after its destruction by Allied bombs in World War II—is the largest Benedictine complex in the world, though today it has fewer monks than it had when Benedict was abbot. The abbey has been destroyed repeatedly over the centuries, sometimes by earthquakes, sometimes by man. It no doubt will be destroyed again, perhaps permanently. The Rule likely will outlive it, as will Benedict's admonitions.

The next morning I walked to Leonessa's bus station, such as it was. There were two routes. I dubbed them, Scottish fashion, the high road and the low road. The low road was the more direct. Take the long driveway from Leo Hotel to the bottom, then turn right and walk a few blocks, going alongside a park. The high road, which I took, departed from the driveway halfway down and went through a residential section. It wasn't that much higher than the low road—perhaps only twenty feet—but it provided a bit of a view before swinging around a corner and dropping to the station, which was nothing more than sheltered benches and two restrooms of the sort one would prefer not to have to use.

I sat on a bench near an elderly woman. I asked her how

long it would take to reach Rieti. She said about an hour, there being several intermediate stops. The bus was due at 8:50 a.m. and arrived on time, this being only its second stop. I sat halfway back, distancing myself from other passengers, and enjoyed the view but felt a twinge of disappointment at not walking—but not too much disappointment because the weather was threatening and I already had made a reservation in Rieti, which was thirty-one trail kilometers from Leonessa. Had I decided to hike, I would have had to hope for weather that was not debilitating and trail tread that was not so muddy as to slow me down. Not wanting to find myself kilometers short of Rieti in the dark, I chose the bus.

At one of the stops a hiker carrying a backpack and a small dog got on. He could have plopped himself anywhere, but he sat directly in front of me. He introduced himself as Erico from Bergamo. He was a physician who also was doing the Cammino di San Benedetto, but he was skipping parts that were too difficult for the dog. Later, thinking back on the rains that were to come, I wondered whether he and the dog returned to Bergamo considerably earlier than he had planned. I last saw him at Rieti's large bus station, where he was met by a friend.

Of all the towns through which the Cammino passes, only Rieti can be labeled a city. Its population is about 48,000. Most of the other towns along the Cammino probably don't deserve to be called towns; for them "hamlet" or "village" might be more appropriate. Rieti sits at the confluence of three rivers, the Salto, the Velino, and the Turano. It has existed at least since the third century before Christ. Its cathedral, named after the Assumption of Mary, was built in 1109 and later was given a Baroque interior (in my experience, such a change usually detracts from, rather than adds to, a church's appearance).

When originally planning my stay in Rieti I hoped to get a ticket for the Rieti Underground tour. On it visitors are shown Roman streets and buildings that lie below the current street level. But I had no time for the tour because I unexpectedly was offered a different sort of tour by my friend Bret Thoman.

I checked into Hotel Europa, where Viviana, behind the desk, was pleasant and her husband, whose name I didn't catch, was sullen. I unpacked, changed my clothes, exited, and walked narrow streets to an open piazza that Bret, unfamiliar with the city, could locate and where he could find a parking place, my hotel being on a dead-end street that was easy to walk to from the bus stop but not easy to reach by car. I got to the piazza first and shortly saw Bret walking toward me.

I last saw him when I made my driving tour of the Cammino di San Benedetto a year and a half before. An American, he lives in Loreto, not far from the basilica that enshrines what is reputed to be the house that the Virgin Mary lived in in Nazareth. Bret founded St. Francis Pilgrimages, a tour agency catering chiefly to Americans. He and his Italian wife, Katia, had me over for dinner. Their children Claremarie and Iacopo were delights, as was Katia's mother, who joined us for the evening and who excelled in everything culinary.

When Bret learned I would be walking the Cammino, he offered to meet me in Rieti, though it would be a 200-kilometer drive for him from Loreto. I put up only perfunctory resistance, and we got together for a day of visiting Franciscan sites. Among them was the Hermitage of Greccio, one of four shrines erected by St Francis of Assisi in the region. The shrine is fifteen kilometers from Rieti and is situated high on a rocky hillside. In the complex's dormitory I was impressed particularly by a low-beamed hallway that ended at a room denominated "Dormitorio di San Francesco." It was little more than a closet-sized cave with a tile floor. Entry was blocked by a corded rope. On a wall inside was a rude cross made of sticks. I surmised that whenever the friar from Assisi stopped for the night, it never was in an establishment rating even one star in the guidebooks.

LIFE ON THE FARM

ON A MAP, Rieti is shaped like a thick, backward-leaning L. Hotel Europa is located near the bottom of the right angle, which meant it wouldn't take long to reach the city limits. In Italy there are no extended stretches of suburbs that make municipal demarcations hazy. At what point does one cross the boundaries of Los Angeles? Driving toward San Diego, nothing seems to change until you reach the empty confines of Camp Pendleton, fifty miles south. If not for the signage, how can you tell when you pass from Tokyo into Yokohama along the Den-en-Toshi Line? You can't. But in Italy passing from city to countryside is quick, often just a few minutes' walk.

The next morning I stepped out of the hotel's nondescript entrance and turned west. I already had become familiar with the first few blocks. At Chiesa San Rufo I took a left into a narrow lane, then a quick right for a block, then a left onto Via Roma. That had me heading south. I passed Mondadori Bookstore, more than a dozen clothing shops, a florist, and a *farmacia*, the sight of which reminded me that, aside from jet lag, I so far had suffered no physical maladies, and for that I was grateful. When you reach "a certain age," the sight of a pharmacy brings to mind such things.

I no longer am young. I ceased being young by the time people in their twenties regularly "sirred" me. When you authentically are young, you're not surprised if store clerks refer to you as "sir." That's the protocol for male customers who seem to have been shaving for at least several years, but at that age no one yet calls you "sir" out on the street because you haven't earned the epithet. You earn it in parallel with the graying of your hair. The exception might be "sir" coming from young boys who have been brought up properly, instructed to address any male notably taller than themselves as "sir."

At some point in later middle age you begin to notice that you are being "sirred" more than you might wish. Straightening your shoulders doesn't help. Even hiding the gray beneath a cap is insufficient. There is something about your gait, perhaps, that indicates that you remember things that occurred before Richard Nixon became president. It doesn't matter if you are slim and athletic, if you run marathons or climb mountains. You're a marked man. Across your forehead is stenciled "sir."

Just past the pharmacy I came to Ponte Romano, which took me across the Velino River. I paused on the bridge, looking upstream and downstream, trying to imagine what someone standing on this bridge's predecessor—the ruined foundations were visible below me in the waters—might have seen and thought. Was crossing the bridge the ancient equivalent of crossing the railroad tracks, passing from the better part of town to the worse?

Before Rome was founded, this region was populated by Sabines. Much of the area was a lake. The Romans drained it and turned Rieti Valley into fertile agricultural land. Prosperity came. From one of the local Sabine families, the Gens Flavia, was descended a future emperor, Vespasian, under whom Rome's Colosseum began to be built. (Its other name is the Flavian Amphitheater.)

The Velino is neither wide nor deep. Its water is smooth, without ripples, and flows as leisurely as the people who walk along it. Through and around Rieti the river makes leisurely curves. The back sides of houses come within a few feet of its bank. The water lies less than a foot below ground level, which suggested to me that either the river doesn't flood or that Reatini are careful not to store anything of value in their ground-floor rooms.

Across Ponte Romano the street changed its name to Via Porta Romana. Immediately I came on the left to Piazza Cavour, another one of those ubiquitous and unimaginative dedications. A minute's further walk along Via Porta Romana would have brought me, sensibly enough, to Porta Romana, now a freestanding structure in the middle of a roundabout. Two millennia ago this was the gate through which one passed to enter Rieti. But I didn't head that way. I walked next to Piazza Cavour, stepped briefly along a curve of Via Salaria (the old Salt Road, connecting Rome and Porto d'Ascoli on the Adriatic coast; not a road made of salt but the road along which salt was transported), and then, following the guidebook, turned south, past a monument to victims of a World War II air raid and through a *borgo* that ended at Via Fonte Cottorella.

Further on the route took a jog to the west, rejoining southbound Via Salaria. Here the path was immediately to the left of the road, separated only by closely-spaced linden trees that provided constant but unnecessary shade on this overcast day. At times the path veered away from the road or dipped into shallow depressions. Usually that meant a little bushwhacking. Here and there thistles grew tall, and I had to push them away to get by. Sometimes I had to divert onto the roadway proper, there being no convenient way to continue along a stretch of path that had become overgrown. While on the road I kept an eye out for drivers, on the assumption that they were unlikely to keep an eye out for me. I returned to the path as soon as I was able. After two kilometers the path turned away from the road and crossed a footbridge. A third of a kilometer later brought me to a dirt road that I took southward for another four kilometers.

The walking was easy and pleasant. Having left the road for another path, I saw no one, other than the occasional farmhand at a distance. I passed a fenced-in field in which chickens pecked for seeds and a turkey showed off his tail feathers. Further on I walked along a field of what may have been dried cornstalks, but they struck me as being too short for corn, yet what did I know about corn, which at home I see only in supermarket bins? Perhaps corn grows short in Italy. Outside cultivated fields the underbrush was uniformly green. Nestled in sheltered spots were bouquets of starry white flowers. I again regretted that my minimal botanical knowledge prevented me from identifying them.

I passed a wall overgrown with a riot of green that indicated not life but decay. On the other side, beyond what once might have been a garden, were the ruins of a building. The right half, three stories tall, was faced with stones. Where they had fallen off the underlying brickwork was revealed—not the stubby red bricks familiar to Americans but thin gray-brown bricks descended from the ancient Roman style. They were seen in profusion at the window openings, in which there remained no trace of glass.

The wooden roof had collapsed, the wood now graveyard gray rather than brown. Weeds sprouted at the open windows and along the roof line, and a vine grew halfway to the roof where the two halves of the building were joined. The left half was shorter than the right and consisted of two stories fashioned of unfaced modern cinder blocks. The lower story was tall and had large openings. Perhaps it had served as a garage for farm equipment. As on the right, this side's roof had collapsed. A few terracotta tiles could be seen through green tendrils that obstructed my view. At the extreme left were three freestanding cinder-block pillars that went the full height of the structure. It was impossible to tell whether they were the remains of a wing that had fallen completely, except for the pillars, or were remnants of ambitious construction intentions that never were brought to fulfillment. They looked like thin versions of the statue-topped pillars in the capital's *Foro Romano*, except they were square rather than round. I fancied seeing one with a representation of Vespasian on top.

The Italian countryside is filled with decayed structures. In some cases, such as around Norcia, the blame can be laid largely on earthquakes. Walls and ceilings shake and tumble, and no one has the wherewithal to rebuild, so buildings are left to moulder. More often, the blame lies elsewhere. Buildings are abandoned—perhaps because of years of failed crops, perhaps because generations of young people moved to the cities to find work—and the buildings' physical decline is more gradual than occurs with earthquakes. Walls are covered and then eaten away by vines that work their way between facing stones and around window frames. Weeds grow on wooden and tiled roofs, their roots slowly pushing, pushing, pushing, until rain seeps in. Tiles lose their grip and slide off. Exposed wood rots, leading to more exposure. The process is slow, relentless, and melancholy. Foolish property tax laws make it more expensive to tear down abandoned buildings than to leave them standing. Taxes are higher on freshly cleared land than on land encumbered with ruins. For many owners, repairs are prohibitive, and demolition and rebuilding are more prohibitive yet. It's a lose-lose situation.

This day's walk looked to be a comfortable twenty kilometers. Despite the overgrowth and ruins, the scenes were lovely, the air quiet, my thoughts unencumbered, at least in the early hours. At my side was the thin Turano, the second-most important river in the valley after the Velino. Beyond the river were fields, and beyond those, where I spotted an occasional car, was the provincial road. As I progressed the sky clouded over, and soon the clouds began to weep. Time for rain gear. I stopped on the road itself—almost half the route from Rieti to Rocca Sinibalda was on pavement—set down my pack and stretched the waterproof rain cover over it. I put on my rain jacket and hoisted the pack, thinking those preparations to be sufficient. I didn't walk far before rain fell more vigorously. I found a spot to step aside, under trees, where the ground still was dry. I removed the pack again and fished out rain pants.

I had had the rain pants for years and had bought them for use in the High Sierra, where August days often see short but heavy thunderstorms. They weighed only four ounces and took up little room, but they were cumbersome to put on, having no ankle zippers. They couldn't be slipped over boots or hiking shoes. Luckily, next to me was a stump. Sitting on it, I unfastened my hiking gaiters and slipped off my shoes, repositioning my feet on them so my socks wouldn't become cluttered with forest duff.

I slid on the rain pants, pulling them over my hiking pants, and brought them up to my knees. Then on went the shoes and the gaiters. I clumsily stood and pulled the rain pants to my waist and zipped up my jacket.

I returned to the road and headed toward the junction where the guidebook said to turn left onto a lane that would become a dirt track. Not liking the look of the runoff, and wary of the mud and the final, steep traverse into Rocca Sinibalda, I stayed on the paved road. It was less picturesque and longer than the designated route, but it seemed safer and certainly cleaner. It took me to the south of Rocca Sinibalda, which first came into view from a long way off. The rain increased in strength. I kept both eyes on my feet, to avoid stepping in puddles or stumbling over stones. For a while I wore rain mittens. They were ultralight and thin, designed to keep rain off but not warmth in, yet soon my hands felt clammy. Perhaps the mittens would have worked better in truly cold weather, but my hands felt as wet inside them as outside them, so I removed the mittens and stuffed them in a side pocket of my backpack. The only parts of me getting wet now were my hands and, when I looked up to see my way, my glasses. My rain jacket's visor didn't extend out far enough to shield the glasses from bouncing rain, so repeatedly I brought up a wet finger to smudge away drops that obscured my vision. The relief always was short-lived.

Trudging in strong rain makes for a dull hike. I had only momentary views ahead. Mostly my eyes saw nothing but pavement and my swinging arms. I could not take in any long views. Had I tried, I would have had a face full of water. I wasn't able to take the phone out of my pocket to check my location by GPS. The phone was certified waterproof, but I didn't trust the certification. I feared an errant drop finding its way through a seam to a circuit just waiting to be shorted out. Years before, on a visit to Germany, I dropped a phone as I slid out of my rental car. The phone fell face down onto the floor of a parking structure, and I picked it up to find a spiderweb of fractures on the glass face. For some inexplicable reason the phone continued to work for the remainder of my trip, but the expectation of its imminent demise forced me to think up workarounds. I didn't want something analogous on this Italian hike. I could have gotten by without a functioning phone, but I already had had enough inconveniences and didn't want to find myself with more.

A few cars passed, most of them going my way. As I heard them coming up from behind, I hunched over, leaning into the hiking poles, and took more hesitant steps, hoping someone would take pity on a hiker in apparent distress and offer me a lift for the remaining three or four kilometers. My ploy failed, so I walked along Strada Provinciale 31 until I reached a crossroads. On the near side was a former convent that now served as tourist lodgings. On the far side was a gas station, behind which was a restaurant. I turned uphill onto Strada Provinciale 32, a thin, winding road that debouched at Rocca Sinibalda's *centro storico*.

Part way up I passed Chiesa dei Santi Agapito e Giustino. The steady rain disinclined me from entering. I wish I had. Back home I learned that the church had but one review at TripAdvisor, and that review was the lowest possible rating, "terrible." The reviewer left no comment. What in the church did he find so inadequate? Whatever the church's condition, I should have paid a visit, for family reasons.

Agapito was the sixteen-year-old martyr St. Agapitus, thrown to the lions in 274 simply for being a Christian. The lions declined to eat him, so he was beheaded. A seventeenth-century statue of him can be found in Milan's Museo del Duomo, where he is depicted as hanging upside down along a pillar, his head still attached and no lions in the vicinity. I can't explain the discrepancy. I have more knowledge of the other dedicatee.

Giustino is known in English as St. Justin Martyr. He was the first Christian apologist—that is, someone whose vocation is to argue against the faith's detractors and in favor of its doctrines. My son is named after the saint, who met his end in 165 and ultimately became the first of several sainted patrons of apologetics.

Justin's *First Apology* was addressed to Emperor Antoninus, asking him to end the persecution of Christians. The request was unfulfilled. Another apology remains, as does a dialogue, but that is all we have from Justin, who was born around 100 into a pagan family. He early developed an interest in philosophy, first looking into Stoicism, then following a Peripatetic philosopher until he tired of the man's persistent request for fees, then turning to a Pythagorean philosopher who proposed a course of study that held little interest for Justin, who at length adopted Platonism. That didn't last either.

One day, at the seashore, he happened on an old man, a Christian, who told him about the prophets and why their testimony was more reliable than that of squabbling philosophers. Justin found the man's argument at first intriguing and then convincing. He adopted Christianity, eventually going to Rome, where he taught and began a school. He disputed with a Cynic philosopher, Crescens, who, according to fourth-century historian Eusebius, denounced him to the authorities. Along with six companions Justin was tried and beheaded.

Upstairs from where I am writing I have a relic of the martyred saint, a tiny chip of bone encased in a brass reliquary. On the wall behind the reliquary is a framed Latin document, executed in 1935 by a notary apostolic, testifying to the relic's authenticity. The *memento mori* is a reminder to me of how few are willing to die for the truths for which they profess to live.

I continued up the hill toward Rocca Sinibalda's *centro storico*. It was in the small piazza there, on my previous trip, that I met tonight's hosts, Federico and Alice Liguori. They have a small farm below the town. I could have walked to it had I turned westward instead of eastward at the crossroads, but I was unsure of my way and thought it best to head to where I had seen them the last time. Once I got there, I would give them a call, Federico having offered to pick me up.

On that prior visit I discovered him and his wife under a canopy in the piazza. It was a market day that is held only once or twice yearly. Dozens of locals were selling things grown or made on their properties. Federico and Alice were selling products from their farmstead, which is called Azienda Agricola Colle Berardino. The name is more mellifluous in Italian than in English: Agricultural Company of Berardino Hill. The Liguoris grow a specialized variety of wheat, which is sold to a co-op bakery and finds its way into Rome, where, they say, it is highly esteemed. They grow chickpeas and other vegetables and produce honey from hives that lie on the far side of their property. Chickens provide them with nine eggs per day—just enough—and, like everyone else in the area, they pick asparagus from the roadside, where it is found in the wild.

They recognized me at once as I approached. Either I was the only stranger in Rocca Sinibalda that day or I looked the part of an American. Likely both. As we talked the wind picked up, and their canopy blew over. We scrambled to right it, and Federico did his best to weight it down. Once the wind behaved itself and the canopy seemed secure, he took me on a tour of the old town, which stretches out languidly along a ridge line and features a castle at the top. The population is 778, according to the 2019 census, but most people live down the hill. I guessed that not a few of the residences at the top were abandoned, a story common throughout the Apennines.

We went first down a staircase to a belvedere that overlooked the valley. Federico pointed to the narrow river far below and said he had a photo of an old painting that showed ships on the river. That was long before a dam was built upstream and the outflow to the valley reduced. No ships could ply the waters now. The dam, constructed under Mussolini, formed Lago del Turano, which sits at 536 meters above sea level and has a surface area of 5.6 square kilometers, making it the largest lake in the region.

We climbed out of the belvedere and walked to the gate of the castle, which is unoccupied except on weekends. The castle dates to 1084. The owner, said Federico, is a professor who lives in Rome. The castle is his refuge from the metropolis. I marveled at how munificent a Roman professor's salary must be, to afford an edifice such as this, or how decrepit the castle must be inside, to be afforded by someone of normal means.

All that was on my prior visit. I didn't stay with Federico and Alice that time. I had a car and was just passing through, having a reservation at a hotel far distant from Rocca Sinibalda. Now, on my walking trip, I reached the piazza where I had met them. Brushed by rain and wind, it was empty. I positioned myself across the way, in front of Bar La Nuvola, and stepped into a recess to get out of the rain. I phoned Federico. He said he'd pick me up in a few minutes. Once at Colle Berardino, I was shown to my room, suitably modest but sufficient. It was immediately next to the kitchen on the ground floor. In the kitchen were Alice and Alessandra, who was working at the farm for two weeks as an intern. She had flown in from San Francisco, where she lived; she said she originally was from Hong Kong.

Later we were joined by other pilgrims, Sergio and Franca. Like the physician I met on the bus, they were from Bergamo. They said they hoped to walk two stages of the Cammino the next day, 14.5 kilometers from Rocca Sinibalda to Castel di Tora and 13.5 kilometers further to Orvinio. They wanted to get an early start, fearing bad weather (which didn't come). The next morning Federico drove them to the *centro storico*, which they hadn't seen, and they departed from there. I ended up leaving the B&B half an hour later, walking directly from the house, taking a back route pointed out to me by Alice.

Everything at dinner had been produced on the farm. For me and the other pilgrims the highlight was a loaf of hot bread prepared jointly by Alessandra and Alice. Sergio took photos of it before it succumbed to the knife. Before Sergio positioned himself for the best shot, Alice placed against the loaf a spray of wheat from the farm. Justifiable pride. Behind us, on the wall between the kitchen and my room, a fireplace gave light and warmth. On the wall above it was the rusted blade of an old agricultural implement. I couldn't tell if it had been a scythe or a saw, and I forgot to inquire.

Lost and Found

The next morning, as I shut the outer door behind myself, I noted the time. It was 8:20. Alice walked with me a short distance, making sure I found the shortcut that would lead me to the rear of the gas station at the crossroads. I wished her and the dogs good-bye and headed downhill at a steady pace. The air was crisp, the sky mostly clear, and my attitude upbeat. I had spent a fine evening with fine people and hoped to return one day to Colle Berardino.

Federico had phoned ahead to secure a room for me in Castel di Tora. He said it was a new establishment, at least in terms of taking in lodgers: a few freshly renovated rooms above a small restaurant called Bar Trattoria Dea. He said I'd find it at the top of the hill on which Castel di Tora was perched.

In half an hour I completed the two kilometers to the gas station and turned onto the road leading south toward Posticciola. I had the way to myself. After another two kilometers I turned onto a step path that went into a forest. Along a stony stretch I came upon ground cover that looked like hedgehogs massing for an attack. The spiky tufts were shades of brown and gray. They looked at once soft and injurious.

I found myself back on the paved road that led toward Posticciola. I could see the hamlet at a distance, but before I reached it I reached its cemetery. Outside the gate was a bench. I removed my pack and stretched. I reached inside the pack and withdrew a snack bar. A few feet beyond the bench was an overlook. In the distance was Posticciola, on a hillside above the valley that the road skirted.

The gate to the cemetery was closed but not locked. On the outside wall was a traditional admonition: "What you are, we were. What we are, you will be." I pulled back the latch and walked in. The cemetery was an elongated rectangle that lay on a ridge at a curve in the road. Immediately to my left was a mausoleum. I scanned the markers and found a poignant one. Beneath a cross was the name Anna Capitani, and beneath her name were her dates. She was born in December 1944 and died the following September. Nothing else was noted. Was she one of so many children who succumbed to a distant war's privations, or had the war itself come into this valley, leaving some of Posticciola's people as victims?

I walked the length of the cemetery, looking at tombs and markers attached to walls or set into the ground. At many were plastic flowers. There was a small chapel, but it was closed, and there were outbuildings where, I presumed, gravediggers' supplies were kept. The place hovered between the serene and the sad. At least it was kept up, more than could be said for many cemeteries in the Italian countryside.

I returned to the bench, hoisted my pack, and continued along the road. In a few minutes I approached the day's intermediate goal, where a sign said "Welcome to Posticciola" in Italian, English, French, and German and noted that the elevation was 572 meters above sea level. The road curved sharply left and then right. On the far side of a small parking area I found the main (at this point, the only) street, which went off to the left. Before me, next to the highway, was Bar Trattoria da Elena. It had a long white awning. A woman walked out—perhaps it was Elena—with her head down. She tended to plants beneath the window. Turning around, she saw and greeted me, and we spoke briefly. She offered to stamp my *timbro*, the pilgrim's credential. Feeling obligated, I went inside and purchased a slice of cake, which I ate standing next to one of the outdoor tables.

With an "ArriverderLa!" behind me, I walked along the middle of Via del Popolo, passing first the post office, then looking at shops, all of which seemed to be closed. I missed the Museo delle Tradizioni Contadine ed Artigiane, the Museum of Countryside Traditions and Crafts—it apparently was the town's main boast—but I lingered over a simple yet handsome fountain halfway down the street. I happily would have refilled my containers there had I needed water. There were two basins, not unlike birdbaths seen in America. Into each basin water spilled from a copper pipe. The pipes protruded from a freestanding, arched wall. At the center of the arch was a shelf on which sat a large pot of red flowers.

The town's name is an amalgam of the names of two towns that merged in 1844, Posta and Roccucciola. In 1876 Posticciola became a district of Rocca Sinibalda, perhaps because it was too small to be on its own administratively. At the far end of the street, raised above the other buildings, was a small fortress, its origins lying in the Middle Ages. I passed below it, following the guidebook's directions and taking a lane that went downhill.

No vehicle access there. On either side were wide stone steps. In the center was a stone ramp, up which bicycles or baby carriages could be pushed with effort. Between the steps and the ramp were more pots and more red flowers. It would have been easy to be overconfident and stumble.

The guidebook instructed me to "follow the directions to the Roman bridge," but I at once became confused. It seemed that I was to turn right onto a short stretch of pavement that passed one house and then ended abruptly at a steep path. I saw no signage and thought I had turned the wrong way. I went back to the ramp and up to the main street and tried again. Yes, it was clear that I had to take the ramp, and at its base the left turn, which followed a line of houses, seemed to go in the direction opposite from the one I should be taking. Seeing no obvious alternative, I turned right again and started down the path, which seemed too overgrown to be the right way.

After descending steeply for a few hundred feet the path became less overgrown, and at a hairpin turn I heard loud gurgling. I found brackish water falling from a rusted pipe into the center of a large tank, which I took to be part of a water treatment system. I continued downhill, a canopy of trees blocking distant views. At length I reached a ravine that ran between the far end of Posticciola and Lake Turano's dam, which I now saw about a kilometer away. The curved dam loomed above me, and before me was a Roman bridge, known locally as the Old Bridge. Beneath the bridge was the Turano River. Actually, this was the successor bridge. Built in the eleventh century, it replaced the original Roman construction.

For centuries the bridge was along the mail route, and over it cattle were herded to higher and lower elevations, as the grazing seasons demanded. I found the bridge to be a gentle arch, the masonry wall on the dam-ward side still intact, the other wall being less sound. The bridge was wide enough for a horse-drawn cart and was covered in grass, except for a narrow, stony strip in the center.

On the far side I came across a warning sign, this one also in four languages, the one with the Union Jack next to it reading this way: "Danger! Possibility of Sudden Flood Waves Also Because of Manoeuvres on Hydraulic Plants." I translated that into English as a warning that the ravine and even the bridge might be inundated if the dam operators released an unusually large amount of water, but above the words was a red-trimmed warning triangle that showed in blue a vast amount of water cascading into the ravine from what looked like a collapsed dam. Perhaps the fear wasn't an intentional release of water by the operators but an unintentional release by a catastrophic earthquake.

Now the path became everywhere green, punctuated by tiny yellow blossoms. The foliage was dense, with trees rising on either side blocking my view of the dam. To my right I heard the occasional car passing high above. I watched my feet more than I watched the path, which became narrower and narrower and overgrown. Thin branches crossed at eye level. Some caught me full in the face. Others I saw in time to push them out of my way. When they caught me or I pushed them, I was splattered with drops from the previous day's storm. The path became ever more congested, and I suspected I had taken a wrong turn. I checked my GPS (I had downloaded the track of the Cammino to my phone before I had left home), and I seemed to be off course. I retraced my steps, again receiving unwelcome showers from the bushes.

This time I watched the path rather than my feet and discovered my error. A yet narrower path had turned off, and I had missed the turn. I couldn't much blame myself, though, since the Cammino's telltale signage—the yellow crossed-*b* on a dark brown background—was misplaced. Instead of being nailed at eye level to a tree at the junction, it was near the ground a little way up the turnoff. One would have to have been looking that way not to have missed it. I had erred but decided the error wasn't my fault.

I continued on, the path now widening, the view opening up, the dam again visible. As I neared its base I found a large metal building. Parked outside was a utility truck. Inside it two workmen were eating lunch. They told me that the gate at the paved road up above was locked. I nodded in understanding and walked on, presuming I'd reach the gate before they would and would wait for them or that they would get there first and leave it unlocked for me. The path had become a gravel road, which turned right onto a sturdy bridge over the river and then left again, close under the roadway. Just before it reached the dam the road made a sharp right and went upward and away from the dam. I paused to get my bearings, and the two workmen drove by in their truck, heading to the gate at the top.

According to the guidebook, "a steep, uphill path on the right takes us back to the road." Did that mean the gravel road the truck had just taken, or was there an actual path here? It took me a little while to see that there was. If there had been a marker pointing to it, I had missed it. I took the path and discovered that the adjective "steep" was accurate. Winded, in a few minutes I found myself alongside the asphalt. Turning left, I reached the dam after a football field's walk. A secondary road passed across the top, headed toward a settlement overlooking the north end of the lake. At a fork I went right, taking a smaller road that hugged the lake shore. It meandered in and out of inlets, with farmland on the upper side and water on the lower.

At one point I heard movement to my left and found, a few steps uphill and behind a wire fence that looked too weak for its assigned job, several white cattle. A large bull eyed me. Had he decided that charging the intruder was called for, the fence would not have delayed him. He could have bounded over it. I said a few soothing words in my best bovine accent, and he turned away to munch on grass. I moved on before he could have second thoughts.

I could not yet see Castel di Tora, which remained hidden around the furthest promontory. Not having my goal in view made the walk seem longer than it was, but my eye was delighted by pink-flowered trees and other colorful delights. Once the town appeared I realized the road would take me around to the back side. As I neared, below me was a moored rowboat, brought as far up the dwindling inlet as had been possible, and ahead on the left were houses. They stood above me behind a tall stone wall, from the upper reaches of which large, woody vines protruded, growing upward to the top of the wall and even toward the houses' second stories. I thought how convenient it must be, on a warm day, to go to the wall and pluck grapes for an afternoon snack.

I came to a junction, where I turned right and could see the back side of Castel di Tora. Two more rights brought me onto the road the circled the town. According to the guidebook, if I followed its serpentine course I would reach the historic center but only after a considerable walk. I noticed a narrow street to the left just ahead. It looked steep but seemed to eliminate the zigzagging. As I approached it I came to a house on the right. The house was situated lower than the road; there were perhaps ten steps down to the ground floor. At the top of the steps a woman chased after a small dog.

"Buongiorno!" I said to her, smiling. She shooed the dog down the steps and returned my greeting. I explained that I was a pilgrim along the Cammino di San Benedetto.

"Where are you from?"

"From America—California in particular."

"Oh, wait! I'm sure my husband would like to practice his English." She and I had been speaking Italian, and I took it that she knew no English. She went down the steps and called into the open door. "Mario! Mario! There's an American here. Come talk to him!"

The husband came up to the street, and we chatted for a few minutes. I gathered they hadn't seen many pilgrims yet this season, it being early, most pilgrims hiking in June or later. My passing by was a bit out of the ordinary. I said I would be staying at Bar Trattoria Dea. Mario pointed down the road I was on, which curved around the west side of Castel di Tora and overlooked the inlet where I had seen the rowboat. "That's the way," he said.

"But I believe I can reach the *centro storico* this way, can't I?" I pointed across the street to Via Turano, a flagstone lane that appeared too narrow for vehicular traffic.

"Yes, you can," he said. "When you get to the top, give my best to Viola." I said I would and waved good-bye. I wasn't a hundred feet along Via Turano before I realized I had made a mistake. It wasn't just steep. It was too steep. My pride wouldn't let me pause for a breather until I was halfway up and out of Mario's sight. I rounded a slight bend and saw, to my relief, a bench onto which I plopped myself. A middle-aged woman came walking down toward me. She carried fruit. I smiled wanly. She smiled in return and opened a door on the other side. It turned out to be Casa Vista Lago or Lake View House, lodging for tourists. I sat for a few minutes more, watching feral cats parade up and down, thinking that towns like Castel di Tora, which is largely depopulated, must have far more cats than people—but far fewer rats than cats.

Having recovered sufficiently, I huffed and puffed to the top of Via Turano, passing under an arch so low that, in olden days, a rider would have had to dismount his horse lest his face be smashed against the stonework. I came out at a small piazza where workmen with a miniature skip loader were tearing up cobblestones. I began looking for my lodgings. I read—or thought I had read—that Bar Trattoria Dea was on one side of the town's main square, on another side of which was the main church. The square was said to have a fine fountain. I was looking for something like the centrally-positioned fountain I had seen in the square opposite the banded church in Leonessa.

I turned uphill, but the road narrowed abruptly and I figured I had gone the wrong way. I turned around, passed the workmen, and took the street the other way. It was called Via Umberto I and weaved right and left and went gently downhill until it got too far downhill. In hilltop towns, main squares are never halfway down the side of the hills, I said to myself. I turned around, realizing that I hadn't gone far enough in the other direction. I passed the skip loader again and this time ignored the narrowness of the street until it reached a dead end in a clutch of medieval houses.

I was at a loss. I thought I had covered most of the old town yet hadn't come across the square, the church, or the rooming house. I returned to where the workmen were putting loose cobbles into wheeled containers by which they would transfer the cobbles to their dump truck, which was somewhere further downhill than I had walked and too large, no doubt, to reach the work site.

"Excuse me, but could you tell me where Bar Trattoria Dea is?" The man in the skip loader silently pointed over his shoulder to the far end of where the cobbles had been removed. I spotted the modest sign above the door. To the left, at the end of the square rather than in its center, was the fountain, through the arch of which one had a grand view of the lake. At the top of the arch, in roman numerals, was the year of construction, 1898. Turning around, I saw across the street the church of San Giovanni Evangelista. Having walked back and forth immediately under its façade, I hadn't even noticed that the building was a church. On Google Maps the square is titled Piazza la Piazzetta, which might be translated as Little Square Square.

Viola was expecting me. She was wearing a long-sleeve black shirt with thin white stripes running across it. Over the shirt was a red puffy. On her head was a white ball cap. On her face was a big smile. She asked if I were hungry. I said I wasn't particularly so, but she instructed me to sit down and had her husband, Angelo, who was back in the kitchen, prepare a plate of cold cuts for me. She went behind the counter and washed glasses. It turned out that Bar Trattoria Dea actually had a bar, in the American sense. Behind her were shelves of bottled spirits.

One of the workmen came in, said to her a few words that

I didn't catch, and went down the hallway to the restroom. I wouldn't have blamed him if he had made a jest at my expense.

Angelo joined me for lunch, as did their daughter Angela, who attended a high school in Rieti. She went there and back by bus, it being too far to go by bike. Angelo said he was a native of Castel di Tora—no doubt a rarity nowadays—but Viola actually was from Albania. When he and I finished eating he took me through a side door and upstairs, where two rooms had been refurbished into guest quarters. The charge for mine was only forty euros, which included breakfast (and apparently the unexpected lunch). The room was well appointed, had a panoramic view of the lake, and, even nicer, had the best towels I had come across in Italy—real towels, large and thick enough to absorb all the water after stepping out from a shower.

MOMENTARILY IN THE SIERRA

AFTER BREAKFAST THE next morning I bid good-bye to Viola and headed downhill along Via Umberto I. At its base a right and then a left got me onto Via Coltodino, which made one swooping curve and then deposited me at the low bridge that crossed Lago di Turano. I estimated the bridge to be a thousand feet long. I had driven over it on my previous trip. Now I walked and had it almost to myself, the road having little vehicular traffic. Just as well, because the pedestrian way was torn up, perhaps for construction, while the narrow roadbed was more walkable.

At the far end of the bridge I came to a tiny oratory dedicated to San Rocco, called either Saint Roch or Saint Rock in English. He had to have been a fine fellow, being the patron saint of dogs and falsely accused people, among much else. He died between 1376 and 1379. His intercession is invoked by those suffering from the plague. The standard depiction of him shows a dog at his feet, with Rocco lifting up his garment to display on his leg scars he received from a bout with the plague. At my own parish

SUN, STORM, AND SOLITUDE

in San Diego, there is a statue of him in just that form, donated years ago by a parishioner who credited the saint with curing him of a serious illness, though I don't think it was the plague.

I peered inside the chapel, the door of which was locked, as it had been when I visited it on my earlier road trip. Wayside chapels in Italy almost always are locked, but at least they're there. I stepped to the other side of the dirt parking area, where there was a half wall. I stood behind it, out of sight of passersby (there were none), and changed from hiking pants to hiking shorts and from a long-sleeve shirt to a t-shirt. The day was warming up, and so was I, and I was about to hike what proved to be the most tiring segment of the journey so far.

Just past the oratory, to the left of the paved road, was a street that aimed sharply uphill for eight hundred meters before turning into a dirt road. The uphill slog was just that—a slog. I passed a few houses set back from the road and then neared a parked car on the left. I could hear voices. My own voice, had I tried to use it, would have been hoarse from breathing so hard on the way up. I paused to catch my breath and to wipe the sweat from my face. Then I went on and found a father and son transferring material from the trunk of the car to a house that lay below street level. I took it they were effecting repairs. We exchanged hellos, and I continued along an incline that was less pronounced than before. After a kilometer and a half from the oratory the road leveled. I passed through a gate, on the other side of which were two short water troughs. At the T-intersection I turned right, the road now—but briefly—being concrete. Soon it became a mere path.

Before it did I passed a fenced-in area with a makeshift cow barn at the rear. It had no walls but only a roof. When they saw me, the cows, with several calves, slowly moved inside the barn and stared back at me. I supposed they didn't see many hikers. Continuing, to my right and far below I could see an edge of the lake and the village of Colle di Tora, which lies opposite Castel di Tora. The hills on the distant side of the lake were verdant, the sky partly clouded, the air now neither warm nor cool.

The path divided into several parts, each going in roughly the same direction. The guidebook assured me that they all led to a hillock, so I chose the widest, which was wide enough for a narrow four-wheel drive vehicle but not much wider. Straight ahead in the distance, on the right-hand shoulder of the tallest hill I could see, was an almost treeless rise. It may have been the logged out area I came across later. The path continued upward gently, making for a ridge line to my left, and then I reached an open area. There the trail fanned out into several tendrils. The ground was open, wide, and gently sloped toward a ridge. Which way to go?

I found in succession two peculiarly positioned Cammino markers. The first was nailed to the end of a long stick. Had the stick been stuck vertically in the ground, the arrow would have pointed to the left, which would have made no sense. To make it point in the correct direction—toward the ridge—the stick was laid almost horizontally, with its end wedged between two rocks. Further up the incline was another marker. This marker likewise was directly on the ground, held vertically by two metal stakes. However unorthodox the positioning, I had no confusion about which way to head: over the grass, dodging stray bushes and trees, toward the ridge line which, as I neared it, I could see featured a tall metal pole to the top of which was affixed still another but larger Cammino marker that pointed to the right.

SUN, STORM, AND SOLITUDE

Once at the ridge I looked closely at the pole and wondered how and why someone would haul it all the way up there. Perhaps it had been brought via the double-track that went along the other side of the ridge; a Jeep could have reached this point. But why such a tall steel pole at all?

Far off to the left, beyond the pole and across the southern arm of Lago di Turano, was the town of Ascrea, which seemed to hang precariously from a hillside. I told myself I someday would have to return and walk its streets. Later in the hike, after rounding another hilltop, I came opposite a similarly situated town located a kilometer south of Ascrea. It had a name that struck me as slightly ominous: Paganico Sabino, to distinguish it from the Paganico in Tuscany.

This Paganico has only 166 inhabitants but its own website. Photos of the town show too many buildings for so few inhabitants. Almost certainly, as in so many small towns along the Cammino, most of the dwellings must be vacant. Ninety years ago more than a thousand people live in Paganico; that seems to have been its historic high point, at least since decennial censuses were kept beginning in 1861. Now only one-sixth as many live there. If I ever get to Ascrea, which is a metropolis by comparison with 240 residents, I will visit Paganico also, despite its name.

I reached the ridge line exactly three hours after leaving the oratory. After looking across the lake at Ascrea I sensed something. There was a familiarity I couldn't quite place. It wasn't the pass itself or the surrounding hills. It wasn't the trees or bushes. It was what lay beneath my feet. Until this day I had hiked on dirt trails or rocky trails, on cobblestone streets or asphalt roads, but now I looked down at a path of decomposed granite and was reminded of the mountains of home. For a few minutes I was back in the Sierra Nevada. It was a Sierra Nevada with the wrong trees and too many of them, but it had the same sort of scattered flowers along the ridge—pinpoints of white, blue, yellow—and the same low, sparse grass, even the same width of view. I turned around, hoping to see Castel di Tora. I saw most of the lake, but the town was hidden behind a tree-covered rise.

I found a downed log and rested. Cumulus clouds were scattered on every side, and above them the sky was softened by cirrus clouds. I sat in full sun, pleasant but not hot, and wondered whether St. Benedict ever had come this way. Probably not, I thought. In his day there was no Lago di Turano, but there was a Turano River. It's likely that travelers walked along it, not high above it. There was little reason to come up here except for the views, and Benedict may have been too busy to have had time for views.

I hoisted my pack and moved on, heading almost due south. Before me was a hill, and before the hill a small herd of cattle, lying directly along the path. I knew nothing about the docility of Italian cattle. Perhaps they were all like Bessie back home, or perhaps they had the temperament of bullring denizens. I wasn't about to go up to them and ask. I skirted them to the left, speaking softly the whole time, letting them know I posed no threat. They didn't seem to care. A few got up and moved away from me. None of them voiced annoyance. I felt relieved once I was past them, and then immediately I came upon a second small herd, which I treated the same way. That herd occupied a junction in the trail, right at the base of the hill. The guidebook said to turn right and go fifty meters to a signboard. I dutifully obeyed.

The signboard was handsomely if rustically constructed. It

held a large, colored map at a scale of 1:10,000. On the right was a list of hiking regulations. Next to them a Cammino marker had been nailed, pointing off the main trail and uphill. The marker was reinforced by a painted yellow arrow at the bottom corner of the signboard. Throughout my hike I saw these painted substitutes for the markers. They appeared on trees, rocks, and other property that didn't seem to be private.

I went in the direction indicated by the arrows. It was along a steep, indistinct, and muddy trail that aimed for an obvious pass. At the upper reaches, near the top, most of the trees had been cut down. Short segments remained—of no use in construction, perhaps?—and the land was mostly open. Was this what I had seen earlier on the right shoulder of a distant hill? I couldn't be sure. I went across the pass and reached a more level area. Widely spaced tire tracks indicated that vehicles had been up here but probably not recently, since the tracks were overgrown. Different species of flowers appeared and soon I began to descend along a dirt road that was largely free of grass. In a few minutes I heard voices but couldn't tell where they came from. Further on the voices became more distinct, and below me through bushes I could see a blue car with its passenger door open and nearby a blanket spread on the ground. I wasn't sure whether I could see those who had been speaking.

I walked on, and my road joined a road that came from the direction of the blue car. At a further junction I had a choice. I could go straight, crossing into a meadow to pick up another path, or I could turn left onto the intersecting dirt road, which first went uphill but then headed downhill toward a main road that led to the next waypoint, the town of Pozzaglia Sabino. But that way was three kilometers longer than the path that lay somewhere ahead of me across the road. The guidebook recommended taking the long way "only if hiking downhill proves challenging." My knees felt fine, so I went straight ahead—and immediately got lost.

This was one of the few places that the Cammino signage was inadequate, at least for someone failing to read the guidebook. I relied on GPS indications, which told me the path was right before me. From the road I walked fifty feet down a gentle slope, and there I found a Cammino marker positioned on the ground. Not suspecting that it might have been jostled out of place, I went in the direction its arrow indicated, to the left. Over a small rise I found a trail, and I took it for several hundred feet. It went further to the left, which seemed to be the wrong direction. I knew that Pozzaglia Sabino, which I had a glimpse of from higher up, was off to the right. There were no markers along this trail, and the further I descended the more suspicious I became. Perhaps the marker I saw in the clearing indeed had been jostled and had misdirected me?

I turned back, going all the way up, but I couldn't locate the marker or the clearing. Frustrated, I continued further until I regained the dirt road. From there I could see the clearing, and I returned to the marker. Working outward from it, I searched the periphery of the clearing but saw no obvious trail, just untrammeled grass. I was about to give up and take the long way around when it occurred to me to consult the guidebook. "If choosing the shorter route, we leave the dirt road for a track on the right that follows a small ridge toward a relay station." The relay station I could see, and I headed across the clearing toward it, even though I saw no trail. It wasn't long before a trail appeared. As the guidebook said, it crossed the hillside beneath the relay station.

I followed a descending ridge, with Pozzaglia Sabino now in full view. There were occasional markers but I would have appreciated seeing more, for confidence's sake. A few times I had to stop and take a wide view, to make sure I was going the right way. At last the trail became obvious; I could see it stretching ahead, all the way to the road that circled the town. First the trail took me away from where I thought I should go, down to a dirt road on the other side of which was a trail going up a hill topped by a large cross. I squinted. It looked like the crossbeam and part of the upright had Christmas lights attached to them. I supposed an illuminated cross must look grand when seen from the town on a clear night.

I turned left onto the dirt road, which soon joined a paved road. In a few minutes I was at Piazza Umberto I, where I found a bench on which I could rest. I watched as sparse traffic went by, moving as slowly as the developing clouds that now filled three-quarters of the sky. I took a road to the left, Via Piana, which descended and reached a junction in front of a house. Following the guidebook, I descended further and then walked along a segment of old concrete that dead ended at a forest. Shortly before the dead end I took a narrow trail to the left, crossed a stream, and found myself, half a kilometer later, before the church of Santa Maria di Maccafà.

Beyond it I passed a melancholy sight, a ruined outbuilding. It once may have been a stable or a granary. The walls were small stones cemented together. The rough roof, now collapsed, had been made of thick branches overlain by thin branches; perhaps thatch had been placed over that, but the thatch was gone. The floor, mostly open to the sky, was overgrown with tall weeds. Structures like this were everywhere in the Apennine countryside. It was hard to tell when they were built and when they were abandoned. They were eyesores and no doubt attractive nuisances to young boys, but it may have been thought too burdensome to tear them down.

The guidebook instructed me turn onto yet another trail. Still I walked in woods. There was no sound—no cars, no birds, no rustle of leaves. A hiker could proceed mindlessly, so long as he watched for stones and roots on the path. A kilometer later I exited the forest and entered the yellow-speckled meadow of a wide valley. On the far side, high on a hill, was my goal, Orvinio. I thought the day's hike was nearly over. I was wrong, quite wrong.

You Can't Get There from Here

EACH TRAVELER TO Italy, after he has spent time in the countryside, returns home with memories of villages that for him represent "authentic" Italy. They are the embodiment of an Italy that once was and perhaps might still be, an Italy where one knows and is known, lives and is let to live, an Italy of olden times and olden buildings, of ochre exteriors and brown-tile roofs, of market days and local dialects and black-dressed widows wearing thick-heeled shoes.

Among such places for me are Castel di Tora and Orvinio.

Castel di Tora is the more impressively situated of the two. It is perched on a steep, freestanding hill and overlooks a large lake. The views are expansive. There is a decidedly and justifiably medieval feel. The place simply looks old, but it wears its centuries well. Its uppermost streets are too narrow to navigate by car. The *centro storico* is for walking, but it doesn't take long to walk the whole of the oldest part of town. As I mentioned, I inadvertently walked it several times.

Orvinio, by contrast, seems spacious though in reality it too is small. A Strada Provinciale bisects it from east to west, and a Strada Regionale cuts it in two from north to south. The town once must have been an important crossroads for commerce, a way station between larger towns in the region. (It is unlikely that anyone ever passed through Castel di Tora just to get somewhere else.) From certain vantage points Orvinio likewise has fine views—after all, it is the highest village within Monti Lucretili Park—and from a distance it sits impressively on its ridge, yet it isn't as picturesque as Castel di Tora. It doesn't exude quaintness. Nevertheless, it settles in my mind as a place eminently livable.

Although its origins stretch back to Roman times (the poet Horace once lived there), the oldest extant buildings go back to the Middle Ages. From that period until 1863 Orvinio had the name Canemorto (Dead Dog). At least that's what a brochure from the local tourist board claims, without explaining the origin of the name. I suppose the dog, even in death, must have been in some way remarkable. The village passed in and out of various hands. For a long time it was part of the Papal States. Before that it was owned by the Orsini family, then by the Duke of Muti. In 1625 it came into the hands of the house of Borghese. Today it is run by a three-man city council.

Eight days after I stayed at his bed and breakfast, Maurizio Forte was elected *assessore*, becoming a member of the town council. He had told me that years earlier he had run for *sindaco* (mayor) but lost because he then was considered an outsider. Even though his father had stayed in Orvinio and had become prominent there, Maurizio was thought to have "abandoned" the village by finding work in Rome. His atonement did not occur immediately upon his moving back. For such a fault reinstatement into a community takes time, but at length he returned to sufficient good graces to become *assessore*, though not yet *sindaco*. That role may lie in his future.

His father produced two books, one a lexicon of the local dialect, another a translation of Dante's *Inferno* into that dialect. Maurizio gave me a copy of the lexicon. Much of it is unintelligible to me. A cabal of local men speaking the dialect in my presence could plot a bank robbery, and I would be none the wiser.

Before political unification, which came in 1861 (though the Papal States weren't incorporated until 1870), there was no nation-state of Italy. There were many Italian states, and within each state, the forerunners of today's twenty regions, there were numerous dialects. In mountainous areas such as the Apennines, where many people never in their lives ventured more than one or two days' walk from their birthplaces, it often was the case that residents of one valley couldn't understand residents of the next valley, the two dialects being so divergent. Imagine a nineteenth-century resident of the Bronx trying to speak with someone from Biloxi—and then double the disparity, to get a sense of the Italian situation.

Maurizio and his wife, Simonetta, had three bed-and-breakfast establishments in Orvinio. The one I stayed at was at the back of their home, on the second floor. They operated under the name Il Sorriso dei Monti, the Smile of the Mountains. It was a particularly apt name because, whenever I was around him, Maurizio was smiling. On my earlier visit to the area, he claimed that all the pilgrims who come to Orvinio are enthusiastic—not a surprising comment from someone who himself is relentlessly enthusiastic.

He said, "I don't like to call them pilgrims," because in Rome the term implies someone who is lost. "I like to call them roaming souls." Only about a fifth of them are Catholic. The majority walk the Cammino di San Benedetto for "spiritual" rather than "religious" reasons, in his estimation. Most who come through Orvinio are over 55; some have been older than 80. Few are of college age. Many hikers are women walking alone. Many who pass through say they are searching for something.

Like his neighbors, Maurizio hopes the Cammino will assist in the reinvigoration of Orvinio. The year before my first visit, about 2,000 pilgrims came through, but so far, he told me, there has been little measurable economic impact. That may come later, but new residents are settling in Orvinio even now. A few foreigners have moved in—likewise, I gathered, some Italians from other parts of the country.

Newcomers, whether from abroad or from up and down the Italian peninsula, have plenty of affordable properties to choose from. By Southern California standards—even by Tuscan standards—the prices are attractive. A renovated 200 sq.m. apartment in the *centro storico* with three bedrooms, three bathrooms, a cellar, and a terrace recently was offered at €160,000, about $180,000. Smaller apartments that need renovation were offered at a quarter of that. Freestanding homes a little way down from the hilltop had similar prices, depending on their condition.

Like other villages in these mountains, Orvinio has been losing population for decades. Young people—like Maurizio himself at one time—are unable to find suitable work locally, so they move to the big cities, chiefly to Rome but also to the industrial cities of northern Italy. By 2008 there were only 470 residents remaining in Orvinio. That was bad enough, but the 2019 census reported only 383. Many houses have become empty, but Maurizio hopes that some who moved away will return, as he did. As they mature and grow tired of the bustle and hassle of Rome—which is hardly more than an hour's drive away—they might come home to Orvinio, if they were raised there. He also sees prospects in newcomers, from elsewhere in Italy or from overseas, who might find in Orvinio the serenity they have been looking for. Perhaps not a few of those newcomers will have come across Orvinio as part of their walk along the Cammino di San Benedetto.

For all its demographic troubles, Orvinio has better prospects than does Castel di Tora. Its population is down to 272, and its proportion of abandoned buildings is higher. Some talk of it as if it were one step from qualifying as a ghost town. No doubt Castel di Tora will have more difficulty than Orvinio in finding new residents. Orvinio is easier to reach by car, it has a larger economic base, and it has those two intersecting highways. People who discover these towns are more likely to do so via highways than dirt trails. But I imagine Castel di Tora may have prospects too, since to foreigners' minds it *looks* like the Italian hill town of their imagination.

When I was two days out from Orvinio, I phoned Maurizio and let him know that I soon was to arrive and to verify that he had set aside a room for me. He had. He warned me that the rains had made the last part of the route to Orvinio—the part skirting the meadow that I now had reached after leaving Pozzaglia Sabino— almost impassable. In the valley the path was flat, and water had turned the trail, where it still was visible, into thick mud and, where it was not visible, into ponds. From where I stood, at the perimeter of the meadow, the trail made a wide clockwise curve, reaching, on the far side, the ruin an abbey. "If this area is waterlogged following rain," said the guidebook, "access the field through the gate and cross it walking toward the Santa Maria del Piano bell tower." That was what Maurizio advised me to do. He said he would send me an aerial photo of the meadow, with superimposed lines showing just where I should go.

I had that map on my phone as I walked along the fence bordering the meadow. The trail was wet but adequate—until it wasn't adequate. Water had accumulated in puddles that were ever larger, until the whole trail was a puddle. I looked ahead and saw the ponds. I backtracked. Where was the gate? I hadn't noticed one. I walked several hundred feet and found it, a place where one fencepost was hooked to another by a loop of wire. I crossed into the field, closing the gate behind me, and found use trails going in two directions. The more distinctive trail headed almost directly toward the bell tower. A lesser-used trail angled off more to the right. It seemed that the most recent footprints were on the more distinctive trail, so that's the one I took.

The aerial photo showed two dirt roads running across the field. All I needed to do was to run into one of them and take it to the right, where they both intersected another dirt road that hugged the far perimeter and, if taken to the left, would bring me to the ruined church. That was theory. It turned out that theory didn't match practice.

I walked toward the center of the meadow, which rested slightly higher than the Cammino and was moist but not wet. Soon the trail from the gate disappeared, but no matter. The going was easy, the ground firm, the wildflowers abundant. I made good time to the far side, but I came across no road. Wherever I was, I wasn't where the photo indicated I should have been. I found myself a few hundred feet from the church—and I found my way blocked. Before me was a stream, too wide to jump even if I could reach it, which I couldn't because separating me from the stream was a barbed-wire fence. I could see, beyond the stream, a small field, and beyond the field the map showed the dirt road that would take me to the paved road. If I could cross the stream, I thought I could be on asphalt in ten minutes, but I had no way to cross.

I turned left and followed the fence line, hoping to find a crossing, even a makeshift bridge. Maybe there would be an opening in the barbed wire. There wasn't. The fence line curved to the left as I passed the church. I followed the curve and saw, sticking out of the meadow in the distance, a metal pole with a sign on top. I couldn't make out the sign, but I presumed it was placed along a dirt road that might get me to the paved road. I turned my back on the church and headed for the sign, which indeed was positioned on a road within the meadow. I walked that road for a few minutes and saw the fence in front of me, blocking the road. There had to be a gate there, and there was. Like the gate that got me into the meadow, it consisted of a section of fence looped to an adjoining post. All I had to do was lift the loop, pull open the gate, step through, and reattach the loop. I could see that just beyond was a transverse dirt road. To the right it went toward where the paved road must have been; to the left it was the impassable portion of the Cammino.

But I couldn't get through the gate. Immediately in front of it the road dipped below the bottom of the fence. The gate stood in a pool of water. Had I tried to pass through, my pants would have been soaked to my knees. The pants would have dried quickly, but my shoes would not have. There had to be another way.

I retraced my steps, returning to where I first came upon the stream. I headed in the other direction. After a few hundred feet the barbed wire ended. I came to a cattle ford where the stream was narrow enough to jump, provided I descended a few feet to its bank. I took a step down and my right foot sank deeply into muck. I nearly fell over. I extricated my foot, but my shoe remained stuck. Not wanting to muddy my sock, I balanced myself awkwardly with my hiking poles and fished out the shoe. The ground had looked firm, but heavy cattle had churned it into thick, deceptive mud. I had to look elsewhere.

I continued to the right and stumbled across one of the dirt roads shown on Maurizio's photo. It went through the stream, but there was a downed log on which I could cross. Once on the other side I looked up and saw, in the distance, two men walking toward the road from the left. One was carrying a basket. Perhaps they had been gathering wild vegetables. They turned onto the road and headed away from me. If I followed them I no doubt soon would be out of the meadow. I quickened my pace but they walked as fast as I did. I called out to them, but they didn't seem to hear. I called louder, saying "I need help!" They turned to look at me but then walked on.

I couldn't walk any faster, so the distance between us never diminished. The dirt road became a dirt trail, and then the dirt trail became overgrown. I passed a herd of grazing cattle on the left. Had they charged me, I would have had no place to run, there being another barbed-wire fence immediately to my side. Ahead the trail curved to the right, and I lost sight of the men. When I reached where I last had seen them, there was nothing. The trail ended at a thick stand of trees. I could find to further trails, not even use trails. Dejected, I turned around, passing the cattle and heading for the road the men had been on when I first saw them. I turned onto it and saw that it went for a long way as it paralleled the stream. Perhaps, I thought, the men hadn't been on their way out of the meadow but on their way in. Perhaps their basket was empty and their goal, whatever it was, was in that thicket of trees where I had lost them. Perhaps I would reach the road to Orvinio by heading toward where they had come from. I did, though the road was as yet unpaved.

I came out next to Santa Maria del Piano, a ruined Benedictine abbey said to have been founded by Charlemagne, who in 817 beat the Saracens in a battle nearby. It's likely that the attribution is incorrect, but the abbey was built in the Carolingian style. It was abandoned in the sixteenth century and so has had nearly five centuries to moulder. Not a few other Italian religious establishments can make the same unfortunate claim.

Several people had just pulled into a small parking area and were headed for the Romanesque remains. I elected not to follow. My passage through the meadow had taken an hour longer than I had expected. I was frustrated and tired. I followed a Cammino marker down the road leading away from Santa Maria del Piano. The guidebook said the few paving stones beneath me were laid down in medieval times. I passed a guardrail above which loomed an overgrown bush bursting with microscopic yellow-white flowers. A little later, on the other side of a fence, there was a large patch of elephant ear plants nestled among baby's breath. I was reminded, for some reason, of the skunk cabbage I see when hiking in the Sierra Nevada, even though that plant's leaves are not shaped like elephant ears.

After a kilometer and a quarter the paving stones and dirt were replaced by asphalt. "We then take a path on the right," said the guidebook, "which, after a final, brief 250-meter stretch, takes us into the village." On my GPS I saw an alternative. The paved road I was on would take me to the same place but at three times the distance. Why make an unnecessary loop? I opted for the path. Another mistake.

It seemed that there wasn't a 250-meter stretch *along* the path but a 250-meter stretch *upward* in elevation gain. At least it felt that way. Each time I came across the wall of a stone structure, peeking out at me from behind thick brush, I thought I was near the top. I wasn't. At length the path became stone steps. I plopped myself onto one and rested. I took out an energy bar and had several gulps from my water container.

Once recovered, I took Via Manenti, which was directly ahead of me. I passed under a fine arch separating the old part of town from the older part of town and found myself in Piazza Garibaldi. It looked familiar. Down the street to the left, just across from Chiesa San Giacomo, was where I first had met Maurizio on my prior visit. This time I would wait for him here, at the piazza. I phoned him to let him know that I had arrived. He said he would arrive in two minutes. I planned on his arriving in five.

I sat on a bench that was against the arch's wall. Above my head was a large signboard touting the Cammino di San Benedetto. Across the piazza, on the right of the continuation of Via Manenti, was a four-story building. The main entry door was under an arch that mimicked the one I had passed under. To the left was the smaller door of a small shop. In its window and on a rack outside were displayed Cammino t-shirts. I would have purchased one, but that would have meant one more thing to carry, and I was in no mood to carry anything extra.

I didn't remember where Maurizio's house was. When he

picked me up the first time, I had parked by Chiesa San Giacomo because that was the only open parking spot I could find. His house seemed a fair distance away, but it really was only five hundred feet away from where I now sat. I could have walked. When we got there Simonetta welcomed me warmly. Their twins, a boy and a girl, were subdued, perhaps intimidated by the prospect that I might speak to them in English. I spoke in Italian, but they remained subdued, so that wasn't it. Perhaps I had interrupted their play time.

There was another lodger, Mario, age 82. He wasn't the Mario I had spoken with at the base of Castel di Tora. Like me, he was a solo hiker. Unlike me, he was largely deaf, which made conversation over dinner difficult. I didn't catch where in Italy he was from. As we ate, Maurizio said how much he enjoyed meeting pilgrims. The prior year he and Simonetta had housed a thousand of them—or did he say two thousand? I don't recall. I mentally calculated that their three bed and breakfasts were rarely without lodgers during the hiking season.

Always happy to assist those on the Cammino, Maurizio said that on many days he put two hundred kilometers on his car, ferrying people here and there. I gave him an opportunity to add kilometers the next day because strong rain was in the forecast. I would be heading for Mandela, where I had reserved a room, and I worried that the weather might make for slow going. The guidebook instructs pilgrims to take a trail immediately to the west of Orvinio. The trail rises into the hills, and I expected it to be a muddy mess, so I had resolved to walk on the highway.

Maurizio volunteered to drive me all the way to Mandela, but I knew that would be out of his way, so we agreed that he would drop me off at the halfway point, Licenza. From there

I would walk. Mario said he preferred to walk the whole way, which for him was only as far as Percile, about a third of the way to Mandela. At his age he saw no reason to try to maintain the sixteen daily stages outlined in the guidebook. The stages averaged nineteen kilometers apiece. If he walked only six or seven kilometers on a particular day, who cared? He was in no hurry.

Ghostly Houses

THE NEXT MORNING we breakfasted to the sound of driving rain. I was glad I had made arrangements with Maurizio. Mario didn't back off from his resolve to hoof it, and he left shortly after the plates were removed. We bid an Italian adieu. I didn't expect to see him again. I lingered for a while, but Maurizio was in no great rush either. The strong rain persisted. I thanked Simonetta for her kindnesses and again praised the previous night's dinner. Maurizio and I got in the car, turned right out of the driveway, then left, then right again and headed onto Strada Regionale 314.

Just outside Orvinio we passed the town cemetery and followed the curvaceous road southwest and then south until it suddenly looped to the north to skirt a ravine. Around the far side was Percile. We hadn't caught sight of Mario. Could he have reached the hamlet so quickly? He seemed spry but not that spry, but who knew?

Now the road went due south and Licenza came into view. Compared to Orvinio or especially to Castel di Tora it was large, with more than 900 inhabitants. We came to a place where the road widened and it would be easy for Maurizio to turn around. He pulled over. The rain had lessened, so I managed to extricate myself from the car and put on my rain gear without getting wet. Once sure that I had all my belongings, I leaned through the window, thanked him, and said I looked forward to meeting up with him again some day. He returned the sentiment, flashed a wide smile, and drove off toward home.

I turned in the other direction and headed out on a road that now had dual names, Via Antonio Gramsci and Via Licinese. I preferred to think of the road in terms of the latter name because of my low regard for the ideology of the Marxist theoretician who, one has to admit, was treated abominably by the Mussolini regime, in whose prison he died in 1937 after a long and pitiable confinement.

The road first turned to the northwest and then corrected itself and turned to the southeast. The land immediately to the sides became more open, with small fields in which young crops grew. Now well below Licenza, I passed Hotel Luisella, which seemed misnamed since it actually was a campground, though a campground with a dance hall. That was the last building I saw for quite a while. I didn't realize that across from Hotel Luisella was a lane that went to Horace's villa. I don't remember seeing a sign for it. The sign would have read "Villa di Orazio." Perhaps I did see the sign and the Italian didn't register, or perhaps, seeing the campground on the other side of the street, I had the impression that this was an area of lodgings and that an establishment called Villa di Orazio was just another hotel. I later saw photographs of the ruins. It seemed that there wasn't much to see beyond foundation stones, yet I wish had spent half an hour walking around the poet's onetime home. Had I consulted the guidebook the night before, I would have been put on notice about this bit of history.

The rain stopped, the sun shone, I was in a good mood (not realizing I had missed Horace), and I made good time. I tracked my progress by watching road signs that listed how far ahead upcoming towns were. On reaching an intersection with such a sign I calculated that I had covered the last five kilometers (three miles) in one hour, a remarkably good rate for me, especially while carrying a pack. I expected to arrive in Mandela early.

I took the route recommended for pilgrims traveling by bicycle. The walker's route, which on this segment was exclusively on dirt trails, first passed high to the west of the road leading out of Orvinio and then, at Licenza, crossed to the east, ultimately entering Mandela from the north. Since I had chosen to walk the road that bicyclists would take, I had to arrive in Mandela from the south, after first going through Vicovaro, the first substantial place I had come to since Rieti. With nearly 4,000 residents, Vicovaro was too large to call a village even if too small to call a city. Neighboring Mandela was a quarter of Vicovaro's size, but that still made it notably more populous than Orvinio, not to mention Castel di Tora.

I walked into Vicovaro and came to the end of Via Licinese (or Via Antonio Gramsci, if you prefer), at the intersection with Strada Regionale 5. Across the road in front of me was a butcher shop. As tempting as the thought of prosciutto was, I turned left, walked past a gas station and past a street with the fine name Via Giacomo Puccini and then came to Bar Zaira, just beyond which I turned uphill on Via San Cosimato toward Mandela. The way was steep and I found myself stopping repeatedly, but I had time, being early. I had called a couple of days earlier to make a reservation at Marzia Febi's bed and breakfast. She seemed a little hesitant until I told her I was a friend of Maurizio. I think that's what got me in. She said she would be out for the day until 2:00 p.m.

When I was almost to her place, a little before that hour, I came across a sheltered bus stop with a bench. I sat down, thinking I should wait before approaching her door, but one minute later a car stopped in front of me, the window rolled down, and to the smiling face I called out, "Marzia?" She nodded, opened the electronic gate, and pulled the car into the driveway. I followed.

The bed and breakfast was called "Febinn," a portmanteau of Marzia's surname and the English "inn." It was a newish building. The ground floor was below street level and had a fine garden in front, with steps reaching it from the driveway, and another entry at the rear of the building. It was on this lower level that Marzia stayed when she was at the property. I gathered that her father lived there. The rooms that were rented out were on the second floor, just above street level. They were accessed from a door opening onto the driveway.

On entering, I first came to a small kitchen. Behind the free-standing sink and counter were floor-to-ceiling windows that occupied the entire street-facing wall. Then I entered the large central room, which featured a fine wooden floor and cases and shelves of bric-á-brac. In a glass cabinet by the window were items fashioned by Marzia herself. During the off season, she said, she made jewelry out of semi-precious stones. When I left the next morning she gave me a Cammino di San Benedetto patch suitable for sewing onto a backpack and a silver pendant shaped like the crossed Cammino *b*.

There were four guest rooms, two of either side of a shared bathroom. I was assigned the room in the right-hand corner. It was large even by American standards, with two beds, two benches, and a side table next to a window that looked toward the neighboring house. I set my pack on a bench and emptied my pockets onto the table. Marzia showed me the bathroom, giving me instructions on how to use the washing machine that was in one corner. I looked forward to cleaning not just myself but my clothes. A window at the rear of the bathroom overlooked a parking area paved in bricks and, past it, a long, narrow rectangle of cropped grass. The left and right sides were framed by lines of tall cypresses, more than a dozen on each side. At the far end of the grass was a balustrade, beyond which could be seen the tops of trees and, beyond them, the side of a tall hill behind which was a bank of clouds.

Marzia handed me keys, one for my room, one for the outer door, another for the pedestrian gate next to the electric vehicle gate. She said she would return in the morning. It was mid-afternoon. As soon as I unpacked, I headed out. It was Saturday, and I wanted to see where the next morning's Mass would be and to verify its time. I also wanted to find a place to eat dinner. I opened the pedestrian gate gingerly. Before letting it click shut behind me, I tried the key. It worked. I would not have been pleased with myself had I left in my room the key that would get me back onto the property.

I turned uphill. I came to a fork, at the tip of which, raised on a stone pedestal, was a large, light-gray crucifix. The corpus was nearly life-size. Directly beneath the crucifix, standing nearly as high as its pedestal, was a fountain with a closed tap, and to either side were confusing European-style directional signs. Two blue-and-white arrows pointed to the right, one to the left. One red-and-white circle indicated no entry, another indicated closed road, though it stood before the metal fence that surrounded the long grassy area enclosed by the roads that diverged at the fork. Attached to the top of the fence was a brown sign noting that Agriturismo Pian di Papa was along the road I was about to walk. It, like Febinn, was a recommended place for pilgrims.

The one-way roads on either side were denominated Via Quinto Orazio Flacco. There he was again, Horace. Near the far end, where the roads converged again, I noticed playground equipment and a sign that gave opening hours for the playground. No one was there. The place was too wet for children whose mothers would not relish immediately having to wash muddy clothes. After the playground I passed accommodations on the left and, on the right, a church dedicated to St. Vincent Ferrer. Then the road, now called Via San Cosimato again, began to climb toward Mandela's historic district.

A tight S-curve went around a small park dedicated to World War II veterans. Within the park a short sidewalk was lined by rows of (empty, I hoped) upright cannon shells. After the next curve I reached a small parking lot, at the far end of which was Nino's Pub. Eight or ten people milled around outside. Google Maps told me I now had a choice to make. I could walk past the pub, keeping to the wall and precipitous drop at the left, or I could take the equally narrow street that turned right immediately before the pub. I turned right.

I passed a closed pharmacy, then a closed post office, and found myself at Piazza Nationale, which had room for only two or three cars to park, though it was the largest piazza in the *centro storico*. At the far end was Pizzeria Il Battaglione. The posted menu seemed adequate. I decided to return in the evening. I went back into the piazza and turned left into a *vicolo* from which I exited next to the church dedicated to Mandela's patron, San Nicola di Bari. I made note of the Mass time. The church door was locked, so I walked a few steps beyond the church into a small square.

There I found photographs taped to the doors of houses. Most of the doors had one. On the nearest door a black-and-white image showed a man and woman standing in that very doorway. The door was open behind them. She stood on a lower step, and his left hand rested on her right shoulder. She had a broad, open smile; his was more subtle. Above them was a title, "We Used to Live Here." Below them was their name, "Familia Valentini Luigi." It was hard to assign a date to the photo, but I estimated it to be from the early 1960s.

The other houses had photos in the same format, each with the same title, each with the names of people who had lived in those houses long ago. Where were they now? Where were their descendants? Behind each door I guessed there to be a house that had not been occupied for a long time. Like other towns I had traversed the last few days, Mandela—or at least its historic district—was as much museum as living community.

I returned to my lodging. As was my custom, I spread out my possessions on the bed, to check whether I had misplaced anything and to remind myself of what I needed to do. I remembered the washing machine and happily took most of my clothes to it. As it did its work, I made notes about the day's journey in my orange, pocket-size Moleskine. There was wi-fi, so I caught up on news but mainly wasted time until the laundry was done. Then it was early to bed.

The next morning I showered, packed, and set my things on one of the benches in my room. I cleaned up the room as well as I could, knowing that new pilgrims were due that day. I locked the door and on a table in the main room, where it easily could be spotted, left a note for Marzia, telling her I was going up the hill for Mass and expected to be back around nine, at which time I'd head off on the next leg of the Cammino.

I found the interior of the small church bright, well painted, and well kept, but in my estimation the sanctuary was overdone. Atop what used to be, before Vatican II, the main altar was a large statue of the risen Christ. He held a banner representing victory over death, and around him was a mass of brown, perhaps formed of papier-mâché, that represented his tomb. On the wall behind, and overpowering everything in the sanctuary, was a robin's-egg blue drapery that hung from, and that obscured much of, a gilded arch. The drapery seemed entirely out of place. I suspected that a priest uncomfortable with triumphalistic expressions wanted to hide whatever was behind it, which may have been the church's premier piece of art.

Below the old altar, on either side of and in front of the new freestanding altar, were potted plants, some flowering, others just greenery. There were more than a dozen pots. The plants showed no unifying principle and added neither beauty nor serenity. High above were chandeliers suspended from a handsomely designed dome the colors of which were dark blue (sky), white (stars), and cream (ribs and miscellaneous ornaments). Given the clutter of the lower part of the sanctuary, I was not surprised to find, halfway down the nave, an array of electric candles. Over the decades I have learned that electric candles are an infallible sign of generalized liturgical and artistic imbecility. Real candles, whether or not of traditional beeswax, are consumed in the very process of burning. That's how it should be. Their being used up symbolizes how someone who prays is "used up" or exhausted through the act of prayer. Prayer takes effort. Electric candles can't convey that symbolism.

Stands of real candles have coin slots, where one deposits enough to pay for a replacement candle. Stands of electric candles have coin slots too, but not to pay for the minuscule amount of electricity needed to keep them aglow until their timers turn them off after a set number of minutes. Their coin slots are for general fund-raising. They're tacky. I would prefer to see no candles at all than to see electric candles. They should be sent to the dustbin of liturgical history, as should polyester vestments.

I settled myself toward the back of the church. A few people already were there, and a few more straggled in before the Mass was half over. I made a head count. There were nine old women and two old men. I was not young, but I was younger than any of them. The priest wasn't Italian, but he spoke Italian fairly well. He may have been Filipino. He had a strong, pleasant voice and hardly needed the microphone that was on the altar, though the women who read the epistle and psalm needed the microphone at the ambo.

I returned to Febinn, expecting to find Marzia, but she had been there in my absence. I knew because the note I had left had been moved. I entered my room and made final preparations for departure. Just as I finished, she returned. She said that Maurizio had phoned her and was bringing several pilgrims. I said I'd stick around. In a few minutes a car pulled up to the gate. Marzia pushed a button to let it in. I told her to let me go to the door. I wanted to surprise Maurizio, who likely thought I already had left, since it now was late morning. As he stepped out of the car, I stepped out of the entryway and greeted him loudly. He laughed and pointed to his passengers. There were two men from Holland, and behind them stood Mario. It turned out we hadn't passed him between Orvinio and Percile. He hadn't gone much more than a kilometer, in driving rain, when a kind soul pulled over and asked if he wanted a lift. He gladly accepted and was off the road long before we came by.

It was raining again, though not yet hard. Maurizio offered to drive me to Subiaco, the historical high point of the Cammino. I looked out the windows, considered what Mario had gone through the day before, and said I would be delighted. Clouds were running low, small ones dipping below neighboring hills. The route to the Sacro Speco at Subiaco was nearly flat, with a descent from Mandela at the beginning and an ascent to the Benedictine complex at the end, but it was nearly thirty-four kilometers. I feared having to walk so far in a downpour. By taking a ride I would miss seeing several minor historic sites along the trail, but I would not the least miss the slog along what promised to be endless muck.

I had a reservation at Hotel Belvedere, which was located on the far side of Subiaco at the base of the road leading to the monastery and churches built into the cliff where St. Benedict once lived. When we arrived in Subiaco, Maurizio lowered the window and, asking a passerby, verified that we were headed toward the hotel. Soon we passed it and half a kilometer later turned onto a road that switchbacked upward. We came to a parking lot, at the far end of which was an arched gateway. Through it ran a flagstone path up to the piazza in front of the Sacro Speco.

Maurizio let me off in the parking lot. The rain was coming down persistently. This time I was unable to don my rain gear and retrieve my pack from the trunk without getting wet. No matter. I knew I was drier than I would have been if Maurizio hadn't shown up at Marzia's. I bid him another good-bye and headed for the arch.

Rise Up and Walk

THE ARCH WAS deep enough to allow me to set down my pack and adjust my clothing, the better to minimize leaks. I knew where I was going. I had visited the Sacro Speco (Sacred Cave) on my prior visit and saw all the public spaces but felt I needed to see them again. Historical sites impress in one way when first seen, in another way when seen later.

From the arch the walkway went straight for a long way. The incline was steady but gentle. Overshadowing the cobblestones were holm oaks. At the end a few steps brought me into the small piazza. To my right was the causeway leading into the Sacro Speco. To my left were restrooms, a gift shop, and a clutch of Boy Scouts chatting with one another, some standing freely in the drizzle, others partly sheltered by an overhang. I turned toward the causeway and looked over the stone wall into the valley above which the multi-leveled buildings were suspended.

Rain spouts protruded from the brickwork in front of me, spilling onto the courtyard below water that had fallen onto the balconies above. The far end of the valley was obscured not by fog but by precipitation. The air was still but heavy. I passed through the narrow door of the Sacro Speco into the covered entryway. On the right were four open arches. By one of them I set down my pack and shook off what water I could. I went to the end of the entryway. On the left the doors to the upper church were closed. I could hear that Mass was in progress. Ahead was the porter's office. The monastery was off limits except to monks and their guests. I turned back and looked down the narrow passageway that paralleled the upper church to its left. It was the roundabout and constricted way into the public spaces. I would take it once I figured out what to do about my wet pack.

I didn't want to leave the pack unattended on the floor next to the arch. I worried about discovering myself pack-less on my return. Neither did I want to trail water through the sacred precincts. I first removed the pack cover and shook off the water. The cover I stuffed into the pack's outside pocket. Then I removed my rain gear and did likewise. That seemed to suffice. Outwardly I was dry, even though there might be some dripping from the rear pocket. I didn't think anyone would notice. I collapsed my trekking poles and put one into each side pocket of the pack, securing them toward the top with Velcro bands. Set to go.

The narrow, rough-hewn passageway ended at steps that deposited me on the next lower level. Before me to the left were stone steps leading up to a landing beyond which were the closed doors of the upper church. I heard a hymn that signaled that Mass was nearly over. To my right were stone steps leading downward and, in a nook, a spiral staircase. I took the latter, which took me to St. Gregory's Chapel, a small room with a bare altar in front of a fresco of the Crucifixion, a window opening to the courtyard into which the spouts had been pouring runoff, and, around to the right, what I was looking for, the fresco of St. Francis of Assisi.

The fresco was painted from life. Francis is depicted without a halo and without the stigmata that he received in 1224. An inscription next to his head reads "*Fr. Franciscus*," in this case "Fr." being an abbreviation for *Frater*, "Brother," another indication that he was alive when the fresco was painted. A marble plaque next to the image says, in Latin, that it was painted in 1223, which would place it three years before Francis's death. To me, the most telling indication is the lack of the stigmata. Francis was the first person known to have received these wounds of Christ. Had the fresco been painted after his death, the stigmata certainly would have been included, as a stellar mark of divine favor. (In our own time, the most widely-known stigmatist was St. Pio of Pietrelcina, known for decades as Padre Pio. He died in 1968 at San Giovanni Rotondo, almost due east of Subiaco near the Adriatic coast.)

Given its age and some overwritten graffiti, the fresco is in fair condition. The colors are faded, but the saint's visage remains powerful. I once read that Francis was said to have had one eye larger than the other. That is what the fresco portrays, the left eye being notably larger than the right. Perhaps the fresco is an accurate portrayal of his face, or perhaps the artist inadvertently showed a disparity that wasn't there in real life, with his error giving rise to what I had read.

What brought Francis to Subiaco? By the shortest modern walking route, his town of Assisi is 170 kilometers away. At a brisk walk that distance could be covered in four long days—not so far for a peripatetic man like Francis. Why might he have come?

In the chapel that houses the fresco, there is a tall, narrow window. On the right is a fresco of the Resurrection. On the left is a fresco of Cardinal Ugolino di Conti, later Pope Gregory IX, consecrating the chapel. Two figures stand behind the cardinal. One of them looks like, and is reputed to be, Francis. If so, then he was present for the consecration, which means his fresco may have been painted at the same time as the cardinal's. In any case, we know the two men were close. It was at the request of Francis that the reigning pope appointed Ugolino the cardinal-protector of the Franciscan Order in 1220.

The parts of the Sacro Speco open to the public are not large in terms of total floor area—the largest room, the upper church, can seat perhaps a hundred—but there are many spaces set at varying levels by winding passages. The layout is confusing. I found myself unexpectedly at the Sacro Speco proper—that is, the cave where the young Benedict lived for three years after leaving Norcia. It is in front of this small room that the entire medieval edifice around me was constructed. When Benedict lived in the cave it was simply that, a cave, set high on the side of a cliff. The exact configuration of the cave, as Benedict knew it, is unknown to us, because parts of it were cut away as the medieval superstructure formed around it. What remains isn't deep enough to have afforded protection from the elements.

The altar in the cave is from the thirteenth century. Its frontal is done in the Cosmatesque style. The floor is similarly adorned. The back half of the cave maintains the rough shape and material of the original. Seated on a protuberance of rock is a marble statue of the youthful Benedict sculpted by Antonio Raggi, a disciple of Bernini, in 1657. Raggi's style closely mimics his master's. The statue seems incongruous. It is bright white against the dark brown of the cave's natural rock. Worse, in my estimation, is that its depiction of Benedict is too soft, almost effeminate. It is not the Benedict one meets in the Rule or in St. Gregory the Great's short biography of the West's preeminent monk. The statue would be more appropriate in a Baroque church, surrounded by Baroque architecture and other Baroque statues.

I went upstairs to the main church, Mass now having concluded. A few people remained, but I had the space mostly to myself. The ceilings (there are several, the vaults having different heights) and walls are covered with frescoes, all in the Sienese style and from the fourteenth century. The larger frescoes show many people packed together—more than forty at the scene showing the Crucifixion. Most of the frescoes are worse for wear, plaster having fallen off, but others look nearly as fine as they day they were finished, even though the colors have faded. One of the most striking is a fresco, located on the left wall, showing Christ at his scourging. He is positioned behind a thin, bluish pillar, with his hands in front of the pillar. You would think his hands would be tied together, but the fresco fails to indicate a rope. That's interesting, but to me there is something more interesting, The pillar matches the one on display in the Chapel of St. Zenon in the basilica of Santa Prassede in Rome. (I write about that pillar near the end of this book.) Whoever painted the scourging scene in the upper church of Subiaco must have known well the pillar at Santa Prassede.

I had been to Subiaco before, on my automobile tour of the Cammino. On that trip I lingered in every room of the Sacro Speco. I stood before each fresco—there are many dozens—looking at them intently, reading what was said about them in a short guide I had purchased at the gift shop outside. On this trip I had the time to linger, having arrived in Subiaco early thanks to Maurizio, but I didn't have the inclination.

From the upper church I walked into what was called the transept but was more like a parallel chapel, located a few steps around a corner from and slightly below the upper church's nave. Its vault was low, every surface richly painted, but not in the Sienese style. Here the frescoes were from the school of Umbria and the Marches. One of the frescoes was of the touching story of the last meeting of Benedict and his twin sister, Scholastica. When it was about time for him to go, she asked him to linger, but he felt duty bound. She prayed that he might be delayed, and suddenly the heavens opened with a great downpour, and he was stuck. The fresco shows them seated at the dinner table in a cutaway view of a room. Rain is pounding on the roof, Benedict has his right hand raised in benediction, and Scholastica has her hands joined in prayer—and a Mona Lisa smile on her face.

At the far end of the transept were double doors, each with twelve small windows. The doors opened onto the courtyard onto which the spouts had been spouting. Here was the Garden of the Ravens, so named because ravens, which featured prominently in episodes of Benedict's life, used to be kept there. On the right side of the transept, as one looked at the doors, were short pews. I made my way to the last one, deliberately. I wanted to sit next to a fresco that I remembered from my earlier visit. I slipped into the pew, set my pack on the floor, and rotated to the left. In the lunette was a representation of the miracle performed by St. Peter, in the company of St. John, as recounted in Acts 3.

"Peter and John were going up to the temple at the ninth hour, which is the hour of prayer, when a man was carried by who had been lame from birth." The man asked for alms. Peter said he had neither silver nor gold but would give what he had. He said, "In the name of Jesus Christ, rise up and walk." Taking Peter's hand, the man rose, astonished and delighted. He "went into the temple with them, walking, and leaping, and giving praise to God."

The fresco depicts Peter and John standing next to one another at the left. John is shown beardless, an indication of his youth, while Peter, wearing a tonsure and heavily bearded, is entirely gray—even though in fact their age discrepancy was not great. They are staring at the man—or, I should say, at the double man, because he is shown twice. At the right edge of the fresco he is seated on the ground. His right hand is raised in supplication. His left hand rests on a wooden support shaped like a miniature sawhorse. Another support lies to his right. His crippleness is indicated by feet rotated crazily backward, toes upturned. Although the conclusion of the biblical account says that the man "was more than forty years old," he looks like a youth.

Between the two saints on the left and the seated man on the right is the man again, but this time post-cure. He is on his feet, which now look normal. He looks up at Peter and John, who, since they are saints, are shown far taller than he. His hands are joined in a posture of prayer, and his face shows mingled fear and astonishment. Behind the two representations of the man is Jerusalem's Temple, in the style of a Romanesque church.

I sat and stared, as I had sat and stared on my first visit. My eyes were drawn, as before, to the twisted feet. I shuddered as I tried to imagine what having a disfigurement like that must be like. I thought of my own disfigurements, which are chiefly not physical. How many opportunities had I been given to "rise up and walk"—and ignored them, even refused them? That afternoon I was weighed down, as still happened on occasion, by the memory of having been betrayed by men I had counted as friends for two decades. Had I let injustice cripple my spirit?

Could I yet rise up and leave that memory behind? Had my Peter and John already come, unrecognized by me?

I gathered up my things and went out. I hadn't spent as much time inside the Sacro Speco as I had thought I would, but I had spent enough. I chose not to put on my rain gear for the walk across the open area to the gift shop. There I browsed the racks of books and pamphlets, concluding that on my last visit I had purchased the ones I wanted. I peered through the glass counter-top at the religious articles and spied something I had been looking for, a small rosary with wooden beads and metal links. I hadn't been able to find a comparable one at home. I could find at home small rosaries or rosaries with wooden beads or rosaries with metal links, but no rosaries with all three attributes. I indicated to the monk who stood behind the counter which rosary I wanted. He opened a cabinet below and pulled out one that was in a presentation box. He opened the box, handed it to me, and asked if I wished to have the rosary blessed. I said I did. Speaking *sotto voce*, he made the sign of the cross over it.

I walked next door to the restroom, put on my rain jacket, and attached the rain cover to the backpack. The rain pants I left in the pack's back pocket because the rain was falling gently now. I thought of taking the steps back down to the flagstone path that I had walked from the parking lot, but a sign at the top of the steps said they were one-way only. I turned around, walked past the gift shop, and continued straight on asphalt, in a few hundred feet reaching a driveway that, down below, was connected to the parking lot.

As I turned left onto the driveway I saw in the distance the Santa Scolastica monastery, named after St. Benedict's sister. It was one of twelve monasteries he founded in the area. Its several buildings sat on a plateau. To the right of the monastery was level land, the back portion covered in olive trees, the near portion open ground. I counted more than a dozen sheep grazing. I walked down to the parking area and followed the winding road through four hairpin turns. A few minutes later the road passed between the olive trees and the monastery, though at that point the olive trees were out of view behind a wall that was at least ten feet high. The road, barely wide enough for two small cars to pass, went through a short tunnel formed by the underside of a three-story tower, the outer wall of which formed part of the wall separating the road from the olive trees.

After that came the parking lot for the monastery, on the far side of which were pilgrim's lodgings that I had considered renting, but I figured I might be tired enough to prefer an actual hotel room, which is why I made a reservation at the Belvedere. Descending from the Sacro Speco, I had guessed that Santa Scolastica was halfway to the hotel, but it wasn't, so it took longer to reach the Belvedere than I had expected. Access from the street was up steep steps and then on a long, inclined ramp with its own switchback. I passed a canopied dining area that, given the weather, was understandably unused. I stepped into the small foyer and realized the Belvedere was less a hotel than a restaurant to which some rooms were attached.

To my left was a large and well-appointed dining room that was not yet open for customers. To my right, behind a glass door and up a few steps, was a bar in which a party was being held. The men wore suits, the women dresses or dressy slacks. At first I thought it was a wedding reception, but then I saw a teenage boy dressed nattily in white and concluded it had been his confirmation day. At the far end of the foyer was a doorway through which

I could see the kitchen off to the left and, directly in front of me, a desk that I took to be for a receptionist. No one was there. I called out, and a man appeared from the rear. I said I had a reservation for a room and gave my name. He said he would be right back, but "right back" turned out to be by the Italian measurement.

At length someone else came out and said he would take me to my room. We went out the front door, past the outdoor dining area, and around to the back, where we mounted steps that went to a building situated behind the restaurant. He opened the outer door, and we entered a sitting area. There were doors to three rooms. The one in the left corner was mine. The room was adequate but nondescript, so understandably I won't try to describe it. I took a two-hour nap.

At a suitably late time I went to the restaurant and promptly was seated. The people I had seen partying had moved to the restaurant and were finishing their dinner, so the air was filled with happy chatter. For dinner my *primo piatto* was excellent ravioli, and my *secondo piatto* was a steak too large to finish. The menu listed it as 3 *etti* (300 grams), the smallest available size. I finished only half and regretted that Italy has yet to discover doggie bags. I was confident, though, that what I left would find its way to the owner's doggie.

Even though I had napped, I slept long that night, a full eight hours, considerably longer than I normally sleep. I couldn't account for it. The next morning I returned to the restaurant for breakfast, which, as is customary in Italy, was included in the price of the room. The selection was wide, and I ate heartily. The waiter was pleasant—a welcome contrast to the man who had shown me to my room. Breakfast done, I cleaned up, packed, and put on my rain gear, for it was coming down with persistence.

Places Seen and Unseen

E VEN THOUGH I hadn't walked all of them, by this juncture I had completed (I use the word advisedly) ten of the sixteen stages outlined in Simone Frignani's guidebook. The next stage was from Subiaco to Trevi nel Lazio, not quite eighteen kilometers. It was to be gently uphill all the way, with most of the journey along the Aniene River.

I headed back in the direction of the Sacro Speco. Near where the first switchback up to Santa Scolastica began, I turned onto a small paved road that went to the right. The road stayed above the river, which at this point was out of sight. The weather improved quickly, and when I came to a picnic area, I plopped my backpack onto a picnic table and put away my rain gear. Neither the jacket nor pants breathed, and I was beginning to sweat. I continued down the road, the asphalt now changing to dirt. I passed a side trail to Laghetto di San Benedetto, but I wasn't interested in seeing the saint's little lake. Soon I came to a hydroelectric plant that lay well below me. Before reaching it I passed a metal gate that was ajar. Beyond the gate I could see nothing but thick foliage. Though tempted to pass through just to see what might be there, I resisted and walked on, coming to a large, grassy clearing at the far end of which was a stone stove that had a wide mouth and a chimney. Perhaps it was intended to be used by fishermen whose days along the Aniene had proved lucky: eat 'em where you catch 'em. Not much further I passed another clearing; in it was a fire ring filled with branches only partly burned.

After a while I found a rock well suited to sitting. I set down my pack and pulled out a snack. I hadn't been hungry back at the picnic table—it hadn't been all that long since breakfast. The rain recommenced, so I took out the rain gear again. Once attired appropriately I looked in the direction I had come from and was surprised to see four hikers heading toward me. Although I had seen hikers at lodgings, until now I hadn't seen anyone else on the trails.

Two of the hikers were human, Paolo and Stella, and two were canine, Leo and Perla, who were small terriers. Each dog wore a harness, and they were linked to one another with a strap. If Leo stopped to sniff something, Perla would walk ahead and unceremoniously jerk him away from the object of interest. Then he would take the lead and do likewise to her. Leo was white and showed dirt; Perla was black and didn't, but no doubt she was as dirty as he. Paolo carried a particularly large pack on his back. Attached to it were two umbrellas, one for him and one for Stella, whose pack was the same size as mine. Both wore short sleeves, despite the chill.

After we had gone a ways Paolo passed an umbrella to Stella (the rain was coming down harder now). He held his umbrella in one hand and a hiking pole in the other. She didn't use a pole and so had one hand free, which she used to drag the dogs into position when they began to stray. Paolo and Stella wore tall gaiters; his were red, hers black. My gaiters were multi-colored but rose only a few inches above my trail runners. Not expecting snow, I had left my tall gaiters at home. The short ones worked well enough for rain.

The three of us (or five of us) walked and chatted, mostly in Italian. We came to an intermittent waterfall that, unhappily for us, spilled its water directly across the trail. It was possible to rock-walk on the side away from the waterfall, but that would have been outside of the dogs' capabilities, so they were picked up by the harnesses and carried across the water like pieces of luggage.

The sun came out, the air warmed, and we stripped down. I put my rain gear away, and they put away their umbrellas. We took advantage of the situation and had lunch, sitting on conveniently positioned boulders. Not long after we finished eating the sun departed and the rain returned, so I again put on my rain jacket and rain pants, and they brought out their umbrellas. The rest of the walk was miserable.

Not far from Trevi nel Lazio the guidebook directed us to leave what was now a paved road and to take a narrow path that went off and upward to the left. I thought the better of it, but they were game, so we said good-bye. The path would enter the town from the northwest. The road would circle to the south and enter from the southeast. My way was longer. I figured they would arrive before I would. They had made a reservation at a place in the *centro storico*. For a reason I now can't remember I made a reservation at a hotel two kilometers on the far side of town. Perhaps I had worried that the in-town places were more rustic than I would have wanted after a hard day. In any case, I didn't expect to see Paolo and Stella again, but I did.

I walked slowly along the road, stopping occasionally to take in a view, once stepping down a side trail. When I returned to the road I found them coming up behind me. They said they had gone only a little way along the designated trail when they came to an impassable, storm-made stream and lots of mud. It wasn't going to be feasible for the dogs, so they backtracked to the road.

The four of them got well ahead of me. I saw from a distance how they maneuvered around large puddles. I followed in their (human) footsteps, but that was a mistake. Wearing boots and tall gaiters, they could venture where I couldn't. At one point I found myself on the opposite side of a pond from where they had walked. My side looked easier until I came to a thorn bush. To keep on the verge and out of the water I had to hold branches back, but one slipped from my grip, and a thorn tore my down jacket. I repaired it with duct tape that evening. In a while I caught up with the others, and we walked the rest of the way to Trevi nel Lazio together, saying good-bye as they turned into the town as I made for the divergent road.

I couldn't figure out why Albergo il Parco was situated where it was. Trevi nel Lazio itself was an out-of-the-way place, even if with 1,800 residents it was sizable for this mountainous region, but the hotel seemed far from anything of interest. Admittedly, I didn't know what was around. Perhaps there were sites of historical or cultural importance. There was at least one that, in retrospect, I wish I had taken the time to see, the castle of the Caetani family, located at the top of the village. It was in this castle that Benedetto Caetani stayed for a while. He wasn't born there. He was born in Anagni, about six hours' walk to the

southwest, but apparently he made a tour of the family holdings. Probably he rode rather than walked, the family being well
off—so well off that he became Pope Boniface VIII, whom Dante
held in such low esteem that he placed him in hell, along with
Boniface's canonized predecessor.

The See of Peter having fallen vacant in 1292, the cardinals,
who were evenly split between Spaniards and Italians, dithered in
electing a replacement, an election requiring a two-thirds majority. Neither national faction wanted to see a pope from the other
faction. The interregnum had persisted for a scandalous two years
when Pietro da Morone, a 79-year-old monk and hermit, wrote a
toughly-worded letter to the cardinals, insisting that divine retri-
bution would fall on them if they failed to elect a pope. By return
mail they replied, "Okay, we elect you." Pietro came to Rome,
refused the honor, but ultimately was persuaded to be crowned as
Celestine V. As an administrator, he was a disaster. He never had
been in charge of other men or of worldly affairs, and he easily
was persuaded by others. He would grant a petition from one
group and then another, opposing petition from another group.
Things were going from bad to worse. It chiefly was Benedetto
Caetani who convinced Celestine to resign, which he did, after
reigning only five months. Caetani became his successor and
took the name Boniface VIII. This was in 1294. Boniface, wanting to insure that his predecessor caused no disturbance, had him
put in prison, where Celestine died in 1296.

In his *Inferno* Dante placed both Boniface and Celestine in
hell, the former by name, the latter by implication. Boniface he
placed there partly for political but also for theological reasons.
The pope had made wide claims for papal (which is to say, for
his own) supremacy over secular matters, while Dante favored a

wide role for the Holy Roman Emperor. Beyond that, Boniface had been accused of selling off ecclesiastical offices, so Dante put him in hell's eighth circle, reserved for simoniacs.

The poet also referred to a pope who made "the great refusal." Most Dante scholars think this is a reference to Celestine, who "refused" to persist as pope even though under duress from those who were supposed to be his loyal assistants. Celestine wasn't the first pope to resign the papal office, but he was the last one until Benedict XVI did so in 2013. Perhaps not coincidentally, in 2009 Benedict went to Aquila, which had suffered a devastating earthquake, and while there visited Celestine's tomb, on top of which he left his own pallium, which represented his authority as the bishop of Rome. The incident was not widely remarked at the time, but many people thought back on it four years later when Benedict announced his own retirement.

I entered Albergo il Parco through the dining room, which was large and unoccupied, except for the proprietor and his wife. Neither spoke English. When trying to communicate with me, instead of using Italian the man opened a bilingual dictionary and pointed to the English words. On learning that I was hiking the Cammino di San Benedetto he gave me directions to Guarcino, which was my goal for the next day. At dinner the pasta was at best adequate, but the *vitello* was excellent. The next morning I had a small breakfast because that was all that was offered. My sleep had been disturbed by several young men across the hall from my room. They were noisy—first with their voices, before they went to bed, then later with their snoring. The thin walls made me grateful for having brought along ear plugs, even though they kept out only part of the noise.

The next leg should have taken me from Trevi nel Lazio all the way to Collepardo. That was how the guidebook had it, but I didn't think I could manage twenty-four kilometers in what promised to be bad weather, so two days earlier I phoned for a reservation in Guarcino, which was at the fourteen-kilometer mark. Unless something untoward happened, I thought, even in rain that should make for an easy day followed by an easier day of just ten kilometers to Collepardo.

I thought it prudent to make this change to my itinerary, but I knew it would alter the remainder of the hike. I would lose a day, one I could not make up later. That meant I would not have time to finish the Cammino at its true end, Montecassino. When making my original plans I had allowed for one day to get by train from Montecassino to Ostia Antica, where I would spend my last night before catching the return flight at Fiumicino. There would be no time to visit Rome proper, but that was all right. I had been there many times. In fact, I used to give tours of Rome, so it was not as though I would be missing a bucket-list item.

Bailing out before Montecassino meant I would miss not one but two legs of the Cammino. I decided not to end the walk at Roccasecca, the penultimate stop on the itinerary, but at the third from the last town, Arpino, from where I would catch a rail connection to Rome's Termini Station. While I would not see Roccasecca or Montecassino on this trip, I had seen them on the prior trip.

At Roccasecca I had been treated royally by Angelo Ciampa, one of the Friends of the Cammino. He spoke no English, but I understood his Italian well enough and his smile even better. We drove to the first church in the world named after St. Thomas Aquinas, who was born in Roccasecca. He is the town's chief boast and a warranted one. The Romanesque church is approached up a long flight of deep steps fashioned by dirt kept in place by boundary stones. The interiors of the steps are half pebbles, half grass. The façade is simple: a double door under an unadorned arch, a small rose window high above, and two vertical-slot windows, one to the left as high as the arch, one to the right placed incongruously higher. They reminded me of prison windows.

Next Angelo took me to the hamlet of Caprile. We hiked upward through it to a small hermitage built before a cave. There was a high wall, as tall as a two-story house, around it and a locked gate. Angelo had the key. The fresco behind the altar was Byzantine in style. The theme was the Assumption of the Virgin Mary. She stood at the bottom center, her arms raised. Above her, floating in a mandorla, was her Son, right hand raised in blessing. On either side of her, each with a halo, stood the apostles. The six on the right included Peter standing closest to the Virgin; the bodies of the six on the left were missing, except for their lower legs, the plaster having fallen away. Centuries ago solitary monks, one after the other, lived in this cave and, later, behind these walls. When did the last one depart—or die? I neglected to ask.

On my earlier trip, after I left Roccasecca I drove to Montecassino. The walking route approaches the great monastic complex from the mountains at the rear. The guidebook says that makes for a spectacular approach. Approaching by car, I had to come up the standard way, along the switchback road rising from the town of Cassino. On that trip too I had the misfortune of rain, but I wasn't surprised because I was there in December rather than in May.

If Montecassino (or, in the American usage, Monte Cassino) is known today, it is known for its destruction during World War

II. German forces were holed up in the abbey, which had a commanding view of the surrounding lowlands. Unable to approach from the ground, the Allies reduced the abbey to rubble by aerial attacks on February 15, 1944. After the war it was faithfully reconstructed, the work taking twenty years. A month after the hilltop complex was destroyed the town at its base, Cassino, met a similar fate. The several battles that occurred at and around Montecassino were said to have taken 120,000 lives, soldiers and civilians together—mostly the latter. In retrospect, capturing the hill hardly seemed justified, since the Allies could have skirted it to continue their advance up the peninsula.

It was the Polish forces who retook the abbey's grounds on May 18. They entered from the north, where today's Cammino now runs. Many of them did not live to see the next day. They lie in the Polish military cemetery, which I found to be the most poignant of all the places I visited on either trip. The cemetery lies slightly below and to the northwest of the abbey. The approach is along a wide, straight avenue lined by trees. It reminded me of the cemetery avenue in the last scene of the 1949 film *The Third Man*.

At the far end is a hillside. Most of the way up there is a grassy area with a large planting bed in the shape of a cross. Between that and the entrance avenue are the graves, set in stone-bordered tiers with gravel between the markers. At the head of each marker stands an unadorned cross. More than a thousand fallen Polish soldiers lie here, in the silence that eluded them in the last days of their lives.

The gigantic abbey of Montecassino, which is home today to only a dozen monks, I found to be cold and uninspiring, perhaps because the day I visited was cold and rainy and perhaps because, that prior trip having drawn to a close, I felt uninspired—or just

tired. I walked the porticoes, visited the lower crypt, saw the
tombs of the brother-sister saints Benedict and Scholastica, and
looked through the small museum and shop, at the door of which
I encountered a female attendant whose visage was as dreary as
the day. The museum featured before-and-after photos of the
World War II destruction but not much else. I thought it not
worth the three-euro entrance fee. The shop had a surprisingly
small assortment of books; this being the largest Benedictine
monastery in the world, I had expected it to offer hundreds of
titles in multiple languages. Aside from the few books there were
herbalist items. Given that Montecassino is nearly depopulated,
I suspected that these concoctions were not made on site.

That occurred on the prior trip. On the second, walking trip I
departed Albergo il Parco in rain. Soon I wondered what had
possessed me to stay there, since I had a two-kilometer walk just
to reach Trevi nel Lazio. This day I would pass from the Simbru-
ini Mountains into the Ernici Mountains, but first I had to pass
through the town, going clockwise through its eastern edges.

Before I got to Trevi nel Lazio I came upon an incongruously
placed bus stop. The narrow metal bench was bright blue; the
backing and curved canopy were dirty Plexiglas. Why was the
bus stop there, so far from any houses? I walked along a fenced
enclosure in which were half a dozen large goats that stared at me
but otherwise seemed unperturbed. Just beyond them I reached
an open area. Across a flower-studded field I could see the top
of a farmhouse. Behind and overshadowing it was a dark-green
hill, the top half of which was obscured by a low cloud. I walked
the periphery of the town, my final steps being down a street
with cobblestones on the sides but six rows of stone pavers in

the middle. The pavers looked slick from the rain, so I took them gingerly. The cobblestones looked even slicker. I was wary because the street sloped toward woods at the far end.

Halfway down the street I came upon an elderly man sitting on a stoop, an umbrella in one hand and a large plastic bag in the other. Perhaps he was waiting for a ride. Not having seen anyone else all morning, I greeted him and he answered brightly. I noticed that he had only a single, shark-shaped tooth in his jaw. He spoke rapidly and unclearly, and I missed most of what he said, but I nodded appreciatively and, when there was a break in what he was saying, I told him I was a pilgrim along the Cammino di San Benedetto. He seemed pleased.

I turned left onto San Teodoro Bridge and crossed the Aniene River. Now I was on a dirt path that went directly west. I followed it until I came to a structure named Santa Maria della Portella. The last word means small door or gate. This had been a customs point between the Papal States and the Bourbon kingdom. Here travelers paid taxes. I paid none, the last customs officer having departed lifetimes ago.

It was little more than a covered space with a niche on one wall. The path ran right through it. No longer a revenue source, it still provided shelter from the elements. In the niche, behind a modern grille, was a *basso-rilievo* image of Virgin and Child. The image, perhaps in sandstone, filled the back wall. Two rosaries had been hung from a horizontal bar of the grille, behind which were several plastic votive-lamp containers featuring pictures of Padre Pio. Set against the carving at the center bottom was a plain wooden cross. On it were draped still more rosaries and, oddly, a pair of sunglasses. To the left of the niche was a bell from which descended a chain. I left the bell silent. Looking up, I saw wooden slats that formed the ceiling. They were painted with simple diamond shapes in several colors. The paint was faded, but it once must have looked cheering.

The path turned due south, aiming for the literal and figurative high point of the day's hike, the Trevi Arch, but I had a long way to go before reaching it. Much of the journey involved finding ways around puddles and mud. I was not always successful. At one point I came upon a non-standard Cammino marker that was nailed to a tree. Perhaps a local had fashioned it. It was a square of plywood painted bright red (the Cammino's "official" background color is dark brown) with a stenciled crossed-b and a stenciled arrow—both in bright yellow—that pointed up. That would have been fine to indicate that a hiker should continue straight ahead, but at this point the path turned right. To accommodate that, the marker was rotated ninety degrees, which meant the crossed b was lying on its side.

The guidebook said that 1.6 kilometers after Santa Maria della Portella I would reach a tributary of the Aniene. At that point I would find a water trough called Capodacqua (Head of the Water) and I would have to wade through the stream to take the path on the far side. I didn't relish having to take my shoes and socks off to avoid getting them soaked. Given the rain, I expected the stream to be flowing strongly, but it turned out to be a rivulet, and I walked across on conveniently placed rocks.

The trail rose steeply. I maneuvered under low-lying, thin branches covered in moss. By this time the rain had ceased so I had one less thing to worry about. The trail became sinusoidal. The green was almost overpowering. Had it not been for the cool temperature I could have imagined myself in a tropical rain forest. Rocks were almost completely obscured by moss and lichen and were lovely in their own way. At length I exited the undergrowth and came not into a valley but onto the shoulder of a hill. The hill rose to the left, and at the right were trees. On either side of me was grass, and before me was a trail that had been worn deep into the soft soil. Except for the bordering grass, it reminded me of trails I frequently have hiked in the Sierra Nevada. They can be treacherous to walk along because they are narrow and deep. It's easy for a foot to catch an embedded stone, even if one uses trekking poles.

All along the trail, but especially here at the higher levels, I had to deal with horse and cow droppings. The latter no longer were simple cow pies. The rain had turned them into cow meringue pies. They and the horse leavings were spread all over the trail by the water. At times it was impossible not to step in them. This was an annoyance, but I knew I would be able to clean my hiking shoes by rubbing them through high grass once I returned to pavement.

I was wearing rain pants now and noticed that the insides had become muddy as my shoes scraped against the fabric. It later would take considerable effort, at the hotel, to clean off the dirt. (When checking in, I tried to hide the mud from the view of the desk clerk, not wanting to be shooed out the door.) Along the trail there was no place to sit down, the area offering no boulders, so I had to rest standing up, and that meant hardly resting at all.

I kept checking the GPS to see how close I was getting to Trevi Arch. I wasn't. It seemed persistently distant. It really wasn't all that far—only eight kilometers or so from Trevi nel Lazio— but the muck and slow going made it seem much farther. I knew it lay atop a ridge, so I kept looking for sky to start appearing behind the trees that now were on either side of the trail. I repeatedly came to false summits, until I came to a junction and looked left. I could see the arch in the distance.

It is an incongruous structure. There is no unanimity on when it was constructed. Some say it was built in the second century B.C., others say a century earlier. It may have marked the boundary between ancient tribes, the Equi and the Hernici, but if so, why? In later centuries it may have been used as a Roman customs station, but there remains no sign of a building that might have housed customs officers.

The arch is made of trapezoidal limestone blocks and is only one block thick. I estimated its height to be twenty-five feet. It is wide enough to drive a car through. It stands by itself, looking forlorn at the top of the ridge. It doesn't have walls extending from it, although there is stonework to the right and left that extends to where the ground rises on either side. Some speculated that the arch was part of a Roman aqueduct, but its shape is wrong—too pointed and not wide enough on the top to support a trough.

Of all the archaeological sites I came across on my journey along the Cammino, the Trevi Arch sticks most in the memory, perhaps because its age is unknown, perhaps because its purpose is unclear. Coming upon it after such a long slog, it looked so gratuitous, though its builders no doubt had a use for it. It must have taken stonecutters several months to construct—not a task to have been undertaken as a lark—but their reason, whatever it was, seems destined to remain unknown to us.

I walked under the arch and down what now was a good dirt road. Soon I came to the paved road that led to Guarcino, a village of many fountains. Before I reached it I confronted a horned cow grazing on the left side of the road, under a cliff. I walked to the other side, where a guardrail kept me from falling into the river far below, and passed her slowly, but she ignored me. A car passed, and she ignore it too. A little further on a driver pulled over and chatted with me, drawn perhaps by my backpack. When we were done, we shook hands, but he didn't offer me a lift. I would have declined, but it would have been nice to have been asked. Then a much younger driver in a red Fiat came by. He didn't stop, but he beeped his horn and gave me a thumbs up.

Soon I was at the outskirts of Guarcino; it had a population of 1,700, but it looked smaller. The town seemed spread out along the road, most buildings hugging the sides, a few situated high above or beneath the level of the roadway. It is said that St. Benedict came through on his way from Subiaco to Montecassino and founded the local monastery. That's possible. An examination of a topographic map suggests that Guarcino lies on what would have been the least arduous route.

Albergo Giuliana was on the near side of town. I turned out to be the sole guest. Dinner was adequate—lasagna without much meat, chicken, chicory as a side dish, bruschetta, cheese, and some cold-cut meat I didn't catch the name of. The rain having stopped, after dinner I walked a bit of the town and located the place where I would depart the road for the trail to Collepardo. Finding it, I returned to the hotel and retired.

Medieval Streets

BREAKFAST WAS THE poorest yet of my trip, merely a packaged croissant and undistinguished cookies. Even the tea was poor. I was glad that the previous evening I had visited a shop where I bought snacks: a real croissant, potato chips, and a pear drink—those formed a supplement to dinner, once I returned to my room—and five of the almond macaroons for which Guarcino is said to be famous. The macaroons I kept for the trail. The guidebook said the recipe for them was "a gift from a monk wanting to repay the inhabitants for their warm hospitality." However that might have been, the next day they proved welcome.

From the hotel I walked into Guarcino, retracing my walk of the previous evening. Where the road began to go left, I turned right, down a flight of steps and into a tunnel that a hiker easily could have missed—in part because it was below street level but mainly because the guidebook I had brought along said "the road takes a sharp turn to the left. Here, before a grocery store, we turn left into a cobbled lane downhill" that, after ninety meters, brings one to Via Santissima Annunziata.

But that wasn't the way I went. I turned right instead of left at the curve because the day before I had spotted a Cammino marker above the tunnel entrance. The next morning I made a beeline for it, not bothering to read the guidebook first—and just as well. The guidebook would have thrown me off. It turned out that the way I went was a recent change to the route. Instead of taking hikers along Via Santissima Annunziata, which skirted the eastern edge of the medieval part of Guarcino, with old buildings on the right and a park and more modern buildings to the left (thus making for a not particularly interesting visual experience), the tunnel led through and between connected buildings and disgorged me into medieval Guarcino. I walked a narrow street that hadn't changed much in a thousand years and, at its end, found myself on steps leading down to Piazza San Nicola, at the far end of which was Chiesa San Nicola.

The interior of the church was magnificent. On a side wall, perched high above the congregation, was an elevated wooden ambo. There were no steps leading to it within the nave. Entry was through a door in the wall; I presumed a passageway behind connected to the sanctuary. The vaulted ceiling was richly decorated and in vibrant colors. The ribs held floral designs, and everywhere there were things to see, many of which, with my inadequate eyesight, I was unable to see clearly, so high up were they, but I could make out ovals containing the heads of saints.

In a side chapel was one of the finest small altars I had seen in Italy and certainly the best of this trip. Behind it stood a large crucifix in front of what looked like a giant marble picture frame, which was the same height and width as the crucifix. Instead of containing a painting, the frame was filled with red damask that made the crucifix stand out nicely. On either side of the frame was a malachite pilaster directly in front of which was a red column, made perhaps of Verona marble. The capitals and bases were of the Ionic order and were gilded, as were several other architectural elements in the side chapel—but not to Rococo excess.

I stepped outside. To the church's right were a wall fountain and an archway leading into a smaller piazza. To the left, on the side of a building, was a locally-made sign for the Cammino just beneath an embedded sign identifying the narrow street as the appropriately named Via San Benedetto. I turned down it, going straight for a few hundred feet, until the pavement turned into wide steps, the better to accommodate the increased grade. On a wall, in English, was a faux-marble sign that said "Welcome to the Medieval Town of Guarcino." The remainder of the street was so narrow that outstretched arms could have touched the neighboring walls simultaneously.

Along the left were alleyways leading to houses that didn't front the street. Down one alleyway I was pleased to see a medieval tower about thirty feet tall. Down another the passage ended at steps that went up to an aquamarine door, to the left of which was a glassed-in niche, framed likewise in aquamarine, that held a statue of the Virgin Mary.

After I passed through a second tunnel, the street ended at an intersection. In front of me was a building with an alcove in which there was a modern mosaic of St. Benedict. Above him an inscription read "*Ora et Labora*." Down the cross street, hanging high on the side of a building, was a sign proclaiming that I was in Contrada San Benedetto, a *contrada* being a municipal subdivision dating back, commonly, to the Middle Ages, but in this case the association was much older, since it was said that

Benedict passed through Guarcino. The building with the alcove once was a small church, but later it became a private home. Around the back, and on a level below where I stood, was the Crypt of St. Benedict, a small room with crossed vaults and a pillar in the center. Frescoes dated from twelfth century, and two paintings were on the walls, one of St. Benedict and the other of the Madonna of Loreto.

The tunnel I had walked through turned out to be Porta San Benedetto, and now I headed downhill away from it and out into the countryside. It wasn't long before I was on a gravel road, and it wasn't long before I began to feel hot, the sun being out and the sky clear. I looked for somewhere to change into shorts. I found a narrow lane off to the right. It promised privacy. I walked down it a hundred feet and stepped under a tree, setting down my pack and clumsily taking off my long pants while standing. I no sooner had I pulled up my hiking shorts than a woman walked by.

I had four kilometers to go to reach the day's midpoint, Vico nel Lazio, a town of 2,200. On one side of the road were terraced hills, each terrace held in place by a stone wall. This was stony land, and the only way to clear it for cultivation had been to remove the larger stones—but what to do with them? What better than to construct walls? It was more sensible than carting them away, which would have been at great expense.

I was on a dirt road called Contrada Menticchio. On either side were fields of olive trees. In some fields the trees were closely spaced, in others they were two or three times as far apart, for what reason I couldn't say. Their gray-green leaves formed the backdrop to the brighter green leaves of the trees that lay sometimes along the edges of the road and sometimes in large clumps further up the hills. I was entering Vico nel Lazio from the north, and the first substantial building I came to was a plain-looking church. It turned out to have two names, Chiesa della Madonna della Grazie (Church of the Mother of Grace) and Chiesa di Sant'Antonio Abate (Church of St. Anthony, Abbot), presumably the desert Father who died in 356. The church was built in the fourteenth century and enlarged two centuries later. It is known for its frescoes but, alas, was locked when I walked by.

I had approached along the left side of the church. Not until I went around the front did I see something curious. Attached to the right side was a half arch made of one course of stone and topped with formed concrete steps. The stones clearly were old, the steps modern. To reach the steps one had to climb a steep, grassy knoll. The steps went nowhere. They ended ten feet up on the wall at a filled-in door. The effect was startling. Perhaps this once had been the way to the choir loft which, within the last few decades, was provided with, say, a spiral staircase inside. It was a pity that I couldn't find out.

I turned left beyond the church and skirted the *centro storico*, something I later regretted. Again I had failed to consult the guidebook the night before. Vico nel Lazio was known for its walls having 25 towers. A church dedicated to St. Michael the Archangel has a Byzantine mosaic, while one dedicated to the Virgin has a crypt dating to Roman times and frescoes from the thirteenth century. I didn't learn about any of this until I looked at the guidebook later. I had plenty of time to wander the old streets—as it was, I arrived in Collepardo early. On my way there, not far from Vico nel Lazio, I passed a modern house with a large front yard. Next to the road was a brick-lined planter, and behind that, on a concrete platform, was a metal canopy with copper-colored rain gutters in what I took to be the Japanese style. Beneath the canopy was a painted statue of Padre Pio, and above him was a large wooden sign that said "Firewood," but there was no firewood. The stigmatist stood by himself.

The rest of the walk to Collepardo was along Strada Provinciale 246, a quiet, paved road. I delighted to find, away from any houses, a patch of wild roses, the only ones I saw on my trip. A little further I walked past the entrance to Pozzo d'Antullo, another thing I missed seeing for not having read the guidebook. It is a karst cave that, in aerial view, looks like a gigantic sink-hole—because that is what it is. Along the edges of the hole the rock has been eaten away, forming a cave, and from the sloped ceiling stalactites hang down. The circumference of the hole is about one thousand feet. A legend has it that the place had been a field, and one day peasants were out there threshing wheat, but it was the Feast of the Assumption, a holy day, and they should have set work aside. The Virgin Mary, angry that her feast-day had been violated, caused the ground to sink and the land to become useless for farming.

Arriving in Collepardo early, I found my lodging, La Corte d'Ivi, easily. It was on Via Roma, next to a post office and over-looking a valley. Across the street from the post office was a botanical curiosity, the Magic Plane Tree of Collepardo. A sign next to the tree said it was a rare example of self-grafting, with one large branch curling around and growing into another. A few steps away, jutting out over the valley, was a sitting area with four benches. At the entry was a fine, large crucifix. I sat on one of the benches, gathering my thoughts, resting, planning the remainder of the day. After a while, although it still was before the regular check-in time, I rang the bell at the bed and breakfast. Ivana Liberatori opened the door and greeted me warmly.

The entry hall had a piano next to the steps at the far end, and on the right was a table with a Hermes manual typewriter, which was there for decorative rather than business purposes. Other tables held other period pieces. I could tell the room had been redone recently. After I returned to the U.S. I discovered that it once had been a little market operated by a man known as "Zio Tom" (Uncle Tom—undoubtedly not with the American connotation).

Ivana led me upstairs. Toward the front of the building was the apartment in which she and her husband, Giorgio, lived with their three children. Lodgers' quarters were through the door at the back, which led across a short bridge to a structure separated from the main one by a gated alleyway below the bridge. The rooms were in a building to the right, but to the left was a large garden, with trees, bushes, lounge chairs, ivy-covered walls, and a profusion of flowers—all this at the second-story level. My room had a small window onto the garden. The room's walls were brick red, the floors tessellated hexagons of brown, tan, and matching red. I plopped myself onto a comfy chair and checked what the guidebook had to say about Collepardo. It was another of those medieval towns with crooked streets and close-set buildings.

I freshened up and went out. At the end of Via Roma I found a bar, where I bought a panino and a can of Fresca. Such was lunch. I stepped outside to lose myself the *centro storico*. Behind the bar I found a small piazza. On one side were a church and the *municipio* or city hall. The triangular piazza was paved with small stones set in swirling patterns, and at the center was a compass rose. I couldn't determine its utility. At airports in America compass roses are placed near runways. Pilots position their planes on top of the painted figures to calibrate their on-board compasses, which have a tendency to fall out of calibration. What was the purpose of Collepardo's compass rose? The only planes that could get there were those hand-carried by children.

I walked by, and occasionally down, narrow lanes that had almost-blank walls on one side and the stoops of houses on the other. Flanking the stoops were potted plants, which also could be found hanging from the walls. Each doorway had a protruding awning. At first I thought the awnings would be too short to keep off rain as one fumbled with a key to get in, but then I realized that the streets were so close together that rain hitting the pavement would have to be falling almost straight down, making the awnings sufficient.

One tantalizing *vicolo* consisted of wide steps—not more than fifteen of them—passing through a tunnel and leading to a door just beyond the end of the tunnel. Suspended from the ceiling of the tunnel was a bright-red bird cage. I wondered whether it had long-term residents.

I turned onto a street with doors, stoops, and plants on either side. There was room for only one adult or two small children to pass. At the far end I saw an arched doorway. It was the Portale del Tolomei, erected in 1606. It was from a time when a branch of the Tolomei family, exiled from Siena, governed Collepardo. Through the doorway was a courtyard that, I supposed, fronted the family's house.

Collepardo's *centro storico* was shaped like an elongated teardrop. Via Roma was on the east side and Viale Guglielmo Marconi, named after the inventor of the radio, was on the west side. I walked along the middlemost street until I was deposited onto Via Roma near my lodgings. I discovered that next to the post office was a grotto built into the fissiparous rock that formed the foundation under La Corte d'Ivi's guest area. The grotto was constructed on the centenary of the apparition of the Virgin Mary at Lourdes. Her statue was in a cavity surrounded by greenery, and lower down was a smaller statue of St. Bernadette. Potted plants, with flowers of lavender, red, and pink, were on either side of them.

Across from my room I met two other pilgrims, Graham and Maureen. They were from Scotland and lived not far from Aberdeen. I told them how much, a few years earlier, I had enjoyed a car trip through the eastern half of Scotland. Aberdeen was one of the cities I visited. My intention had been to follow the route that Samuel Johnson and James Boswell took in 1773 on their famous visit north of Hadrian's Wall. Each wrote an account of the adventure, Johnson's being titled *A Journey to the Western Islands of Scotland* (1775) and Boswell's *The Journal of a Tour to the Hebrides with Samuel Johnson LL.D.* (1785, the year after Johnson's death). Aberdeen was one of their early stops as they went counter-clockwise, beginning at Edinburgh.

The day still being young, Ivana offered to take the three of us on a tour of the Certosa di Trisulti, a one-time Carthusian charterhouse. Located a few minutes' drive from Collepardo, Trisulti superseded nearby monastic works, was consecrated in 1211, and became a national monument in 1873. Like other religious buildings, it is owned by the Italian state. The origin of the name is in dispute. For centuries the place was run by the Carthusian order, until in 1947 the prior was shot dead within his quarters. After an investigation the local order was disbanded, the monks being dispersed to various other monasteries. They were replaced by Cistercians, whose numbers persistently dropped until, when we visited, only one octogenarian monk remained in the giant complex.

Ivana was an accomplished guide but she spoke little English, so I translated for Graham and Maureen. She showed us through the areas that were open to the public (about three-fourths of the place was off limits). From a balcony we looked down upon a handsomely crafted garden maze, and the monastery church was stunning, with a frescoed and rounded ceiling depicting *The Glory of Paradise* (painted in 1683 by Giuseppe Caci) and much fine artwork, from various centuries, on the walls and on the iconostasis separating the public areas in the front from the monks' areas at the far end. The overall style was a subdued Baroque.

Next we went to the monastery's eighteenth-century pharmacy, which featured trompe-l'oeil frescoes. The pharmacy faced what once was a botanical garden where the monks grew herbs needed for their medicines. On a wall was a wonderful painting showing caricatures of two men, one rich and one poor. The rich man wore fine clothing and had a protruding belly. His face was fleshy, and he had a supercilious smile. The poor man's clothing was ill-fitting and dirty. His hunchback mimicked the other man's abdominal extension, his face was thin, his smile almost accusatory. His index finger pointed toward the rich man's vest.

Back in Collepardo, Ivana took us to an herbalist shop. She knew the proprietors well. It was run by the Sarandrea family and specialized not just in herbal medications but in fine liqueurs. The present owner's son, Simone, was there along with his cousin, Enrico. Simone explained to us, in good English, that upstairs was the laboratory in which they manufactured their offerings. The shop was most famous for distributing the sambuca created originally by the monks at Trisulti. As a brochure mentioned, the family took particular pride in noting that "in 1961 Pope John XXIII authorized the Liquoreria M. Sarandrea to use the title of Provider to the Vatican State."

The four of us sampled two liqueurs and were much pleased. I asked Simone about the differently colored boxes on the shelves. The boxes, dozens and dozens of them, contained varying combinations of herbal extracts. He said the contents of the green boxes were derived from whole plants, while those in the blue boxes came from only the youngest segments of the plants. Bidding Simone and Enrico good-bye, we returned to our rooms.

A little later Graham, Maureen, and I sought dinner, but the only place open was the bar at which I had had lunch. All the restaurants were closed, this being Collepardo's closure day. It worked out well for us. The bar's proprietor recognized me, no doubt appreciating that I had brought other paying customers, and treated us well.

Misplaced Trust

THE NEXT MORNING I departed with Graham and Maureen. She had only a day pack but didn't carry it. Graham had it strapped to the back of his backpack. The total volume on his back approximated what was on mine. By this time I knew well that I had over-packed, though not disastrously so, but I nevertheless was surprised that the two of them could manage on so little. Maureen explained that she had back problems and could carry almost nothing, so they were forced to go light. Along the Cammino they had been making good time, some days walking two whole stages, about forty kilometers, despite the irregular weather.

Just outside Collepardo—which is to say only a few minutes' walk from La Corte d'Ivi—we left the road that led to Trisulti and hiked uphill to Via Santissima, which we took until we reached the church named Santissima Trinità. But we didn't reach it together. Graham and Maureen were moving quickly, and I struggled to keep up with them. The day already warming up, I wanted to take off my long-sleeve shirt. I paused at a wayside shrine and told them to keep going. We were expecting to wind up at the same place for the evening, a religious house in Casamari, and I said I'd see them there. By the time I put my shirt into my pack and got moving again, they were out of sight.

Now walking more leisurely, I got to the church and turned onto a dirt path that led downhill for half a kilometer until it reached a stream, which I crossed on a Roman bridge. On the other side the path rose persistently until it reached a level spot where I unexpectedly found a picnic area, cordoned off behind downed logs. At the far end was a large metal cross of modern vintage, and along the perimeter there were rustic wooden benches. I sat and ate a snack. The sky was almost cloudless, the day now warm. I noted a rock with a carved inscription. It turned out to be a date, 1925.

Rested, I returned to the trail, which I had to myself and to my thoughts. I recollected how frequently I had thought about not thinking while hiking.

To avoid injury, you have to maintain a certain level of awareness on a trail, more so than on asphalt or concrete. You have to look far ahead occasionally, to make sure you're still on the right path and that nothing carnivorous is blocking your way, but mostly you look at your feet, to make sure you plant them rightly. This means your vision doesn't extend much beyond your height. If, like me, you commonly using hiking poles, their use immediately falls into a regular rhythm that is coordinated with your steps. Your legs go right, left, right; your arms swing out, back, out; your eyes look down, down, and occasionally up. Once the parts of the body are set in motion, it takes no concentration to keep things going. Your mind hardly is needed, so it has two options. It can occupy itself with something else, or it can occupy itself with nothing.

Sometimes my mind does the former. I have composed entire public speeches while hiking, but that is rare. More commonly I think through, repeatedly, tasks that I need to perform—what must I do to finish the research on *that* book, how long will the writing phase take, how long will the editing phase take, when can I expect the book to be published? That sort of thing. Equally often my mind is at rest while my body is in motion. Call it mental suspended animation. For me this can be a welcome relief, since I probably don't rest my mind enough in the course of a normal day. I never watch television or listen to radio, things one can do without having to think at all. I do go online each day, and that tends to be low-intensity time, in terms of mental load.

With each passing year I find it takes more mental energy to read. I read a lot but not nearly enough. I'm unable to forget Samuel Johnson's remark that a young man can make something of himself if he reads five hours each day. I no longer am young and no longer have the endurance to read that many hours day after day, but I'm acutely conscious of my need to do something like that, lest I die ignorant. (As for making something of myself, I fear that possibility escaped me decades ago.)

So, as I said, while hiking I thought about not thinking, and then I thought about things that I now don't recollect. I just walked. It went for well over a kilometer, mostly uphill, through woods that weren't thick enough to block out the light. The trail ended at the road to Trisulti, where I found another picnic area and two small chapels, one on either side of the pavement. From a distance they looked like guards' stations. Each chapel had a locked latticework door through which the interior could be seen easily. I put down my pack on the protruding foundation of the right-hand chapel and ate the last of the macaroons I had brought as snacks. I saw that one of the largest trees in the picnic area had a complex root system reaching out along the ground. Its lower trunk was half obscured by lichen, and its wide canopy no doubt gave summertime visitors a welcome break from what otherwise could be a brutal sun.

I got up to stretch and went around to the chapel's door, peering in. On the far wall was a marble pedestal. Atop it was a crucifix to which I told my troubles and wishes. The response I received was not audible, but it was sufficient. I hoisted the backpack and moved on, now along the road. In less than two kilometers I reached Trisulti. Across the road from the entrance, at the edge of a wide spot in the pavement, lay a large dog, taking in the sun. Just beyond the entrance was a fountain, where I refilled my water containers.

I hadn't walked far beyond the fountain before a portly cyclist caught up to me. He paused and we spoke for a few minutes. He mentioned that this had been the coldest and wettest May in two decades. I believed him, wished him well, as he wished me well, and I watched him pass beyond the trees. Soon I came to a sign pointing toward the ruins of the San Domenico monastery, which was founded in 996. I didn't take the side journey. I was beginning to worry about how long it would take me to finish the stage's twenty-five kilometers. I hadn't been impressed so far this day with my speed and knew I had no chance to catch up with Graham and Maureen.

Two kilometers later I passed the ruins of the convent of San Nicola at the village of Civita. The road curved around a valley, and Trisulti came into view in the distance. From this vantage point the size of the monastery could be appreciated. It was surrounded by thick forest and lay on the slope of a large hill. It looked more like a fortress than a place of prayer, though I suppose even fortresses, when used for the purposes for which they were built, become places of prayer, at least until the bombardments cease.

The road ahead of me had long straight sections interrupted by curves. On either side were fields, one with what I was sure was young corn, another with what I was even more sure were four horses. As I walked by, the four looked at me but otherwise didn't move. (The corn paid me absolutely no attention.) After that I came upon a field of tall grass. Scattered through it were red poppies, yellow daisies, and bright blue flowers that I couldn't identify. At the far end of the field, on a little rise, was a ruined stoned building. It was a beautiful view, marred only by a telephone pole off to the right.

After I walked a particularly unpleasant section of dirt road, the pavement returned and I found myself at a junction at a hamlet called Santa Maria Amaseno, Amaseno being the name of a stream that I crossed on a bridge. At the junction a sign for Abbazia di Casamari pointed to the right, along a wide road. On the other side of the junction was a thin lane going sharply uphill. Its name was Contrada Case Cristini. I consulted the guidebook, which said the lane gained elevation for half a kilometer before reaching "a cluster of houses," and then, within less than half a kilometer the surface changed to dirt and for nearly a kilometer the way went "up and down through olive groves" at which point pavement returned. After that came more dirt for about two kilometers and then periodic dirt until, after another five kilometers, the town of Casamari was reached. Casamari was the day's goal, for I had a reservation at a religious house.

At the junction I had a decision to make. Should I follow the guidebook, which would lead me chiefly along dirt roads, or did prudence suggest that I stick to paved roads instead? Earlier it had been raining, though not hard, and I expected the dirt roads ahead to have been transmuted into muck. Looking at the map on my phone, I saw that taking larger roads would involve walking a greater distance, but probably I could walk considerably faster on them than if I clomped along muddy trails. I opted to stick to the pavement. I would trust Google Maps to show me the way.

It turned out to be misplaced trust.

At the junction I turned right, and the road that seemed wide at the junction passed a few buildings and became narrow. No matter. This was the way to go. The sign had pointed this way, and the sign was meant for motorists. I came to a turnoff for the town of San Francesca but continued straight. This took me further away from the guidebook's route, but, looking at the map on my phone, I could see that the road I was on would get me to Colleberardi, which was most of the way to Casamari.

I walked along pruned hedges and past light-industrial buildings. Houses were scattered up the hillside to my right and below me to my left. Most of the roofs of the latter had loosened or even missing tiles. Occasionally I would come to a house built within the last thirty years, but most of them were much older. I made good time, only infrequently encountering a car. Sometimes, on this day and others, I timed the intervals between cars. Rarely was it less than ten minutes; often it was more than twenty.

After a while Google Maps directed me to turn onto a thinner road that angled more directly toward Casamari. The road I had been on, had I taken it further, would have swept to the west before turning again to the south and finally to the east, where Casamari lay. The new road brought me through areas that were even less populated. I came upon a field with a lone occupant, a mangy horse. The road became thinner yet. There no longer were long straight stretches. I walked by several houses, turned right and then left onto other lanes, and found myself at a farmhouse outside of which wandered several goats. One had a remarkable black-and-white speckled coat. I never before had seen such markings on a goat, and I later regretted not taking photos of him.

The lane ended and became a trail that descended sharply downhill. The trail was encroached upon by plants of various sorts until it deposited me in a small, overgrown field, at the center of which the trail abruptly ended. I checked my phone. I still was on Google Maps' route, but the route had disappeared. What I saw before me was not what the screen indicated I should see. I should have seen a trail that met a road that apparently was paved, but there was no way, absent bushwhacking, to get to that road from where I was. I evaluated my options. I could force my way through the undergrowth, hoping to make my way to the road, which was some distance off, or I could turn around and find a transverse road that would take me eastward toward a road I was sure would get me to Casamari.

I chose the latter. I retraced my steps, going back up the path, back up the hill, back to the goats and then right and left, right and left along several paved roads until I came to a rise from which I could see Casamari in the distance. Above me, behind a wall, was a house, and a woman was near the wall, tending olive trees. I asked her the way to Casamari. She said to go straight ahead, then turn right. I did that and came upon a man working on a piece of farm machinery. I asked him the same, and he pointed ahead, saying I should take the road toward Scifelli. Part way there I came across the Cammino route and turned onto it.

Signage along the way was not optimal. At one junction I was unsure which way to turn. It took me a few moments to locate the Cammino marker, which had been attached at shin level to a rock that partly was obscured by foliage. From there on the center of the path was filled with puddles, and I had to walk on the verge. I passed fields covered with thickly-growing grass out of which, here and there, popped brightly-colored flowers, red poppies among them. I came to pavement and took it the rest of the way into town and to the monastery, where I arrived shortly before rain commenced.

There was a long driveway from the street to the building, but I wasn't sure which side to enter. Was this the back or the front? I walked past the monastery to the far side, to see if there appeared to be a proper entranceway. There wasn't. I returned to the driveway and saw a woman pulling weeds in the grassy area that fronted the street. I asked where the main entrance was, and she pointed up the driveway. I walked to the top, found a front door that looked like a back door, and rang the bell. After a long wait the door opened. Sister Giuliana showed me to a room almost above the entryway. The accommodations were modest, as befitted a religious house. There was no true shower. The long, narrow bathroom had curtains that could be pulled to divide it into thirds, with the sink at one end, the toilet at the other, and a floor drain in the middle. The middle part became a make-shift shower. It was awkward, but it worked. No towels had been provided, so for the only time on my trip I used the travel towel I had brought along—and discovered that it wasn't absorbent.

Now clean, I organized my belongings and heard voices out-side. Opening the window, I saw Graham and Maureen heading out to dinner. I joined them. We ate just down the road at Ristorante Caio Mario, the sign for which I initially read as Ciao Mario. I made sure to say "Ciao!" as we left the restaurant.

Graham, Maureen, and I were the only guests at the monastery, and we may have outnumbered the nuns. Aside from Sister Giuliana the only one we saw was Sister Annette, who was from Africa. The next morning I wanted to settle my bill. At breakfast, which was served in a room opposite a small chapel, I told Sister Giuliana that I wanted to pay. She motioned me into the hall and opened the door to the chapel. My pronunciation must have been poor. I had said *pagare*, but she must have heard *preghiere*: pray rather than pay. My bill was twenty euros, for room and breakfast. I handed her thirty, thanked her, and said a final good-bye to Graham and Maureen.

Homage to a Mandolin Maker

THE WEATHER PROVED fine the whole way to Arpino. Clouds threatened rain, but I stood up to their bluff and they backed off. By this time I had had my fill of stormy weather and was pleased at the prospect of having my last day on the trail be meteorologically tranquil.

This was a moderate-length stage, slightly downhill for most of the first five kilometers, then mostly level until one stiff, two-kilometer stretch near the end. The route began a few minutes' walk from the religious house, at Casamari Abbey, a Cistercian establishment built in the Gothic style. The Cammino was entering more congested lands now, and it must have taken Simone Frignani no small effort to lay out a route that maintained a rural feel.

After leaving Casamari I entered onto a long stretch in, through, and adjacent to wide, untilled fields in which flowers of blue, red, yellow, and white pushed up through the mass of green, like prairie dogs poking their heads out. In the distance was a highway, but at my feet were narrow lanes more suitable for bicycles than cars. Buildings were few; views were wide.

I came upon a melancholy but common Italian sight, a building half-built and abandoned. This one was three stories tall. It consisted only of concrete pillars and crossbeams, a completed roof, and brickwork enclosing the ground floor. Around it weeds grew with abandon. In my imagination I saw the story: a farmer's ambitious expansion following several years of high-priced crops, then the bottom falling out of the market or the farmer falling ill and perhaps dying. I was reminded of the parable of the rich fool told in Luke 12:16-20. A rich man, having an abundant harvest, tore down his barns to build larger ones in which to store the surplus grain, expecting thereafter to enjoy a leisurely life—only to learn that "this night thou must render up thy soul."

Not long after, I intruded on a woman feeding her chickens. They were in a makeshift pen formed by stringing chicken wire around the remaining pillars of a structure that once might have been a garage. She didn't notice me, so intent was she on looking after her charges. I went on my way silently. Not long after that the Cammino passed under a motorway, which it paralleled on the other side for a while, before passing back under to the original side. Another two kilometers brought me to Castelliri, with 3,400 inhabitants an exurb of the larger Isola del Liri, where 11,400 lived. I hardly had entered Castelliri when I heard what I took to be a bullhorn, and I caught sight of the tail end of a red car as it moved down the street. On the roof were angled plywood boards forming two signs. They were too far away for me to read, but I guessed they were touting a candidate for local office. Later I saw a flatbed truck. A large sign in its bed proclaimed the merits of a candidate named Fabio Something-or-Other. Below his large image were mug shots of a dozen other people, perhaps other candidates from his party—or perhaps his opponents. I couldn't tell. Like the red car, the truck blared out campaign slogans.

Between the two sightings, while walking through a close-packed neighborhood, I came across a chapel. Above the door was a sign, dated 1949, that said the chapel was a gift "to the inhabitants of this valley" from Giustino Palermo, who wanted to provide them a place "they may gather in faith and in prayer." Plaster was falling off the uppermost part of the façade, and balustrades on either side of the steps to the front door were partly broken, yet the chapel still seemed to be in use. On the porch were two potted plants, both looking healthy.

Once I got to the end of the neighborhood, and before returning to the larger streets of Castelliri, I came to a chain-link fence on the other side of which was a packed dirt area next to a house. Various construction tools, such as a small cement mixer, sat forlornly. Around, in, and under the tools were ducks, geese, and hens. I spoke to them through the green-wire fence. They responded with indifference, so I departed. The route only briefly took on a rural look again; Isola del Liri was not far away. I knew I had reached it when I saw next to the road a sign that said, "Isola del Liri, City of Music, Twinned with New Orleans, USA." In the center of the sign was the New Orleans city seal. I wondered what Dixieland might sound like with an Italian accent.

I walked along Isola del Liri's main street for several blocks. At one point I came upon a house that sat six or eight feet below street level. Between the house and the road was a small garden, and at one end of the garden was a plastic niche in which stood a plastic statue of Our Lady of Lourdes. For a country now mostly irreligious, there remained many signs of a religiosity that once was, and in a few quarters no doubt still is, vibrant.

I arrived at the first bridge over the Liri River. Concrete embankments on either side held in the water, which flowed slowly over several weirs. On the far bank a bland-faced apartment building towered over the scene. I looked in vain for what I was told was a magnificent waterfall and wondered whether to find it I needed to walk upstream or downstream. Then I remembered that the river split into two arms on reaching the town. It likely was along the further arm that I would find the waterfall. I walked on, past shops of all sorts, along a road now crowded with cars—something I hadn't seen since Rieti.

After a short walk I came to the second bridge and found what I wanted. Far upstream but in full view was Cascata Grande. At eighty-eight feet high it would not be mistaken for Yosemite Falls—it lacked the grandeur of great height—but it spilled a wide expanse of water into a green basin that narrowed only slightly as it became the river over which I stood. The waterfall was to the right of a stone building that looked several centuries old. Beneath that building the cliff was a thick mass of green, both trees and ivy. The guidebook informed me that Cascata Grande was the only Italian waterfall found in a town center.

I crossed the bridge. To the left was a restaurant with covered outdoor seating. I wasn't interested in a full meal, so I turned my attention to the shop next door, a gelateria. I ordered a cup with three scoops: mixed berry, hazelnut, and strawberry. Stepping to the side of the river, I sat on the rim of a large planter, my pack at my feet and the cup of gelato in my hand, and watched the water flow by slowly, to the subdued sound of the distant waterfall. It was a welcome respite.

Not quite full, I decided I would walk a few blocks and then purchase a sandwich at a bar. I passed one bar immediately and skipped it because it looked the worse for wear, but I soon regretted doing so, since it was the last bar I saw until I entered Arpino. Not far from the river the road forked, and I went left onto Via Nazareth, a road worth walking just for its name. It took me past the municipal *calcio* stadium, the sight of the bleachers reminding me of high school football stadiums back home. I had reached Isola del Liri's town limits and entered a rural area.

I came to an intersection labeled on the map Vallefredda (Cold Valley). There were a few scattered houses but nothing that looked even so large as a hamlet. The guidebook said to take a side path. I did, and after a few minutes it deposited me on Strada Provinciale 92, here called Via Collecarino (Cute Hill), which I took southeast toward Arpino. I saw nothing particularly cute, and I couldn't determine why the valley through which I walked might have been considered colder than areas around it. Perhaps surveyors who took measurements and proposed names, decades ago, were here during a wintry storm. That might account for the name of the valley but hardly for the name of the hill.

Deciduous trees no longer had an exclusive claim to the route. Large pines took over in many places as the road ascended. At this point the ascent still was gradual. It would not be gradual for long. At one point I came across a large sign touting Hotel Il Cavalier d'Arpino. I had stayed there on my previous trip and understood it to be the premier hotel in Arpino. Located close to the *centro storico*, it was an easy walk to the places I wanted to visit. I looked forward to staying there again but, again, I had delayed in making a reservation. When I phoned two or three days earlier, I learned that all the rooms were spoken for.

The stiff uphill segment brought me high above a valley that was more densely filled with housing than I had expected to find it. I feared I would lose the elevation I had been able to gain, powered as I was by the sugar in the gelato, but the road leveled out and widened, and the rest of the way into Arpino was nearly flat. I came into the town from the north, a high concrete wall to my left, an expansive view over the valley to my right. Cars now were parked cheek by jowl along both sides of the road, but on the valley side, on the other side of the parked cars, was a wide pedestrian promenade, along which I strode with pleasure, now confident that I would not become a traffic statistic. A road came down the hill on the left side and joined the road I flanked, and the two merged only for a few paces before ending in a piazza, at the far end of which the asphalt gave way to modern paving stones and the way became so narrow that two cars would have had difficulty passing one another. I was entering Arpino's *centro storico*.

The buildings were dull yellow or dull orange or duller gray, but the overall effect was one of light. From second-floor balconies hung greenery, some still in flower, the flag of Italy, and the ensign of the local *contrada*. I passed another gelateria, but it was closed—and just as well. I needed real food. Shop windows proclaimed *sconti* (sales) up to fifty percent off, but I wondered whether the sales were permanent, since the displays looked old and worn. Soon I was in the Piazza Municipio. Two millennia ago this was the site of the Roman forum. A fenced-in area at the center still preserved the original Roman pavement.

Arpino may be known best as the birthplace of three famous Romans: the statesman and orator Cicero, the consul and general Marcus Agrippa, and the general and statesman Gaius Marius (the "Caio Mario" of the restaurant in Casamari). Much later the town saw the birth of the Mannerist-style painter Giuseppe Cesari, known as Il Cavalier d'Arpino because his patron, Pope Clement VIII, made him a Cavalier of Christ. It was in Cesari's studio that Caravaggio was trained for about a year, before he went elsewhere, and it was after Cesari that the Arpino hotel was named.

To my left as I entered the piazza was a church dedicated to St. Michael the Archangel. On my previous visit I attended Mass there. It was a chilly December morning. Strewn throughout the church were space heaters. Those in the know arrived early to sit near them. The church was packed—an unusual sight in today's Italy, but I concluded it was because during Mass three infants were baptized. Most of the congregation likely were relatives who hadn't entered a church since they last attended a baptism.

I remembered seeing near me a man in a wheelchair. I took him to be a paraplegic. I couldn't tell whether he managed to get to Mass on his own or had someone assist him. He reminded me of a younger man I see on Sundays at home. His mother brings him to Mass. He has a severe palsied condition, perhaps also mental disabilities. His mother, who is in late middle age, wheels him up at Communion time. She receives, but he is unable to. The priests bless him, and he's wheeled back. Each week I marvel at the mother's loving dedication to her son, and I wonder what will happen to him when she is gone.

At the far end of the piazza, opposite from where I entered, was Arpino's city hall, a modest building of three stories. You had to look carefully to see the sign "Municipio" near the top. It was here, on my prior visit, that I found something I was searching for.

In most quarters Arpino is known best as the birthplace of Cicero. To me it is best known as the birthplace of Luigi Embergher, one of the most famous mandolin luthiers of all time. He crafted instruments that were considered a step up from the instruments made by the best luthiers of the late nineteenth and early twentieth centuries. Silvio Ranieri, perhaps the best mandolinist of the early twentieth century, would play nothing but Embergher instruments in concert. He compared them to the work of Stradivarius.

Ranieri was twenty-six years younger than Embergher. One day he visited the latter's shop in Rome and tried out a mandolin labeled "Gold Medal Paris 1900." He was so impressed that he offered to buy it. Embergher said it wasn't for sale but offered to let Ranieri use it in that evening's recital. After the performance Embergher offered the instrument to Ranieri as a gift. Little wonder, then, that the two remained friends until Embergher's death in 1943. The luthier's work was continued first by a father-and-son team, Domenico and Giannino Cerrone, with the elder taking over Embergher's work in 1938, and then by Pasquale Pecoraro, the last to build using Embergher's precise standards and methods. Pecoraro died in 1987. Since then, Embergher mandolins—particularly those made by Embergher himself—have become prized possessions of top classical mandolinists and not a few accomplished amateurs.

I'm neither. I took lessons in the classical mandolin repertoire for several years, but my skills never exceeded those of an interested beginner. I own several mandolins, including one similar to those Embergher produced at his atelier. Despite my deficiencies as a player, I thought it proper to pay homage to Embergher and so sought out the museum dedicated to his work and containing the forms and tools he used to make some of the best instruments in European history. That museum was in Arpino. It was called Museo della Liuteria.

I found the museum a two-minute walk from Piazza Municipio. It was on the main road through town, Corso Tulliano ("Tulliano" referring to Marcus Tullius Cicero). The place was locked at the front gate. I came by later and found the front gate open. I crossed the garden and headed into an open doorway, but I couldn't find any indication of a museum. At length I asked someone where its door was and was told the exhibits had been moved—apparently temporarily—to the *municipio* itself, so I returned to the piazza. On the second floor I found what I hoped was only a fraction of the museum's holdings. The room was small. On the perimeter were display cases, some having carving tools, others having partly-formed mandolins. Ten chairs had been set up—the maximum possible, given the tight quarters—and at the far end of the room the evening's performer was tuning his instrument. I wasn't able to stay long, but then there wasn't much to see.

That was on my earlier visit. This time I left the piazza and headed for my hotel, which was a long walk away. I passed the official location of the museum and walked along Corso Tulliano to where it squeezed through what once must have been the gate to the upper city. The name of the street changed to Via Vittoria Colonna. I passed a church dedicated to St. Anthony and a butcher shop right next door, and soon I was at Hotel Il Cavalier d'Arpino. I sighed that I hadn't been able to get a reservation there. I kept walking. I came upon another church dedicated to St. Anthony. This one specified that the honoree was St. Anthony of Padua, the saint relied upon to find lost articles, which led me to conclude that the other church likely was dedicated to St. Anthony the Great, the Egyptian monk, but I didn't backtrack to check.

I had passed out of the historic center of Arpino and had entered an area where buildings were spaced widely and had no attractive architectural features. All was modern. My walk was persistently downhill, and at length I curved around well below the museum, the upper floors of which I thought I could discern on the ridge above me. My hotel, Il Casale della Regina, stood isolated, sheltered in a thick copse of trees and thus out of sight of the main part of Arpino. I walked up the long driveway and found a young man lounging on the porch above me. I greeted him and took the steps toward the front door. He asked if I were a guest. Finding that I was, he stood and introduced himself as Massimo. He was the desk clerk. His duties that day must have been light, since I seemed to be the only guest.

Later, when he laid out a light and late lunch for me, I asked about the best way to get to Frosinone, which I expected to have to reach to find a train to Rome. He advised me to take a Cotral bus. The name stands for Compagnia Trasporti Lazio. The company operates the inter-urban routes in Lazio. I already had done some research and planned to take a train from Arpino's tiny station, but Massimo said the bus would be better. It didn't sound better to me; besides, I wasn't sure just where to pick up the bus and could imagine my getting on a bus headed in the wrong direction. That night at dinner, the daughter of the owner said I should take the train, so my initial plans were confirmed.

After lunch I washed some of my clothes in my room's sink. That done, and the clothes set out to dry, I headed up the hill, back to the *centro storico*, and took in part of the town, but I didn't return to the museum. Although I carried no pack and so traveled light, by the time I finished my evening constitutional and was back in my room, I discovered that I had mirror-image blisters on the balls of both feet, just behind the big toes. These were the only blisters I had received on the entire trip, and I thought it odd that they should appear on an easy, pack-less walk. But no matter. The next day I had only to walk to the Arpino station.

It turned out to be a longer walk than I had expected. The way to the station was roundabout. There may have been a shortcut used by locals, but Google Maps didn't offer it to me, and I would have been a little suspicious if it had, given the wild goose chase it sent me on when I tried to reach Casamari. I allotted forty-five minutes for the walk, and that ended up being about right.

I turned off the main road (such as it was) onto a narrow lane that seemed wrong by its width but right by its name, Via Stazione. On one side of the road at the junction was a farmhouse overgrown with vines. On the other was an outbuilding propped up by two stout poles—not the place to be sleeping, I thought, if there were an earthquake. This was to be my last time to walk in the Italian countryside, so I paid attention to the olive groves to my right and the low stone walls to my left. The road ended at a faded yellow building that bore no sign. The top floor appeared to be a residence. The bottom floor had a wide tunnel through the middle. On one side were benches, and on the far side was the platform and beyond it a pair of tracks. There was no ticket booth and no attendant. I would have to pay once I got on the train.

Already waiting were two tourists (English as I recall) and a local man. The tourists were headed in one direction, I in the other. They seemed to know which train to take, so when theirs and the local man's train came I stayed behind, waiting for the next train, which I hoped would head in the opposite direction. It did, I got on, and I paid a last glance toward Arpino and the Cammino di San Benedetto. At Frosinone I changed trains for Rome, and it wasn't long before I reached Termini Station.

WHERE ALL ROADS LEAD

I WOKE TO YET another dreary day. I could hear rain cascading down the air shaft onto which my small room's sole window opened. At least I could look forward to a shower that I could complete without banging my elbows against the stall's sides. Although I'm tall, I'm not wide, yet I repeatedly found myself banging my elbows on the walls of Italian shower stalls, some of which were smaller than phone booths—a comparison that might be hard for me to prove now that phone booths are extinct. I never have understood why Italian hotel rooms don't provide shower stalls that are just a few inches wider in each direction. There almost always is sufficient room. It can't be out of a desire to save water, since taking a shower in a constricted stall takes longer than in a stall with maneuverability, and a longer shower means more water used. At least at Hotel Lirico, in Rome, I found a properly proportioned shower stall, and I gave silent thanks to the architect.

By this time I had become inured to the standard Italian breakfast. It's fine for a few days, but then culinary boredom sets in. I had had similar feelings in England with the standard English breakfast of overcooked bacon, sausage ("bangers"), eggs, grilled tomatoes, mushrooms, toast or fried bread, and tea. That's far more than I ever eat for breakfast at home—when visiting Britain I never lose weight—but, after a week or two, you crave variety. I had variety at some of my Italian lodgings, but most served up the Mediterranean equivalent of the English breakfast. At least with the latter you get lots of meat and so lots of protein. In Italy the meat consists of a few Bible-paper-thin slices of prosciutto or, worse, of ham that likely came from the packaged lunch-meat shelf at the market. Mostly breakfast consists of cakes, croissants (*cornetti*), and cereal.

The weather had clearly up somewhat, with only a gentle drizzle. I left the hotel and headed toward the Spanish Steps, with my first stop being Palazzo Barberini, a seventeenth-century palace. Its land had been a vineyard when, in 1625, it came into the hands of Maffeo Barberini, who later became Pope Urban VIII. The plan was to enclose a pre-existing structure. Like many plans, it expanded, a foretaste of government projects of our own time. Urban assigned three architects to the project: first Carlo Maderno, who then was working on the nave of St. Peter's; soon Maderno was assisted by his nephew, Francesco Borromini. When Maderno died in 1629, the commission went to Gian Lorenzo Bernini, who was a sculptor more than an architect, but the young man also was a prodigy. Construction was completed in 1633. After Urban's death in 1644 the property was confiscated by Innocent X (more on him shortly), but the palazzo was returned to the Barberini family once Innocent died. One adjective never associated with the palazzo, I'm sure, has been "modest." It's a gigantic structure of 120,000 square feet, with 187 rooms and eleven staircases. The overall footprint is that of an H.

Palazzo Barberini today is home to the Galleria Nazionale d'Arte Antica. "Antica" signifies that the museum features works produced prior to 1800. Although I had been to Rome many times, I never had been to this museum and looked forward to it. Among other works it includes a Caravaggio (*Judith Beheading Holofernes*), Raphael's *La Fornaria* (*The Baker*—actually, Raphael's mistress), and Hans Holbein the Younger's portrait of Henry VIII, this being one of many copies, the original having been destroyed. It is the well-known portrait of a squarish Henry, age 49, well bedecked in his finery and with preposterously wide shoulders. By this time Henry already was somewhere between fat and obese. Holbein gave him a fairly flat abdomen, so that may explain the exaggerated width: to preserve the king's overall volume.

One of the most striking pieces in the Galleria Nazionale is *The Vestal Tuccia*, carved in marble by Antonio Corradini, who died in 1752. The life-size image is of a young woman—a vestal virgin who lived secluded in the *Foro Romano*—who is covered completely by a shroud. Only her hands and feet, plus one lower leg, are exposed, but much of the rest of her also seems exposed because the sculptor somehow managed to make the shroud diaphanous. Although her head is covered entirely, you can make out the mouth, nose, and closed eyes. Similarly for the torso. It is almost as if she is wearing Cellophane. (She surely would require a second layer to be fit to appear in public.)

In another part of the Galleria I came upon an image at which I couldn't help laughing. It was by Filippo Lippi and is called *Tarquinia Madonna*. Painted in 1437 in Lippi's unmistakable style, with fine lines and great detail, it shows the Virgin Mary holding the Christ Child. It's a beautiful painting, except the Child is a pink-faced Charles Laughton.

After an hour and a half I left the museum and found a place to sit on the rim of a non-functioning fountain in the courtyard. Children were running about, and harried-looking tourists were coming and going up and down the curved drive that led to the street. I was tired but looked forward to having, for the first time on this trip, an actual lunch—and more than a lunch: a feast, but not an Italian feast. I was headed for Babington's.

In 1893 Anne Maria Babington and Isabel Cargill—two English spinsters—went to Rome to set up a tea room that would bring a bit of the home country to the many British visitors to Rome. They set up on a small street near Piazza di Spagna but soon moved to the establishment's present location, at the foot of the Spanish Steps, on the ground floor of an eighteenth-century building. Babington's is on the left side as one looks up from Pietro Bernini's sunken-ship fountain, Fontana della Barcaccia, toward Trinità dei Monti church at the top of the steps. (Pietro was Gian Lorenzo's father.) On the right side of the Spanish Steps is the house where John Keats lived and, in 1821, died. I never have visited that house. By the time I get myself to Piazza di Spagna, I always have more interest in tea than in Keats.

At Babington's I asked for a table for one and found myself sitting next to an English couple. They had but a day left in Rome, they said (or did they say they had only one day in Rome? I forget), and they asked me how they should spend time around their hotel, which was situated not far from where I was staying. The woman had difficulty walking, and they sought nearby attractions. I recommended Galleria Doria Pamphilj. It's on Via del Corso, around the block from Piazza Venezia, where, from a high balcony, Mussolini used to cajole his crowds. Few visitors seem to know about the Doria Pamphilj. I never have seen it crowded, never have had to wait more than two minutes to purchase a ticket.

I told the English couple that, in the old days, when I used to guide groups through Rome, I reserved the Doria Pamphilj for the last day, by which time most of the tourists had been "museumed out." When they heard that I was taking them to yet another museum, one they never had heard of, they were reluctant. "Trust me on this," I always said. Once we had gone through the museum and were back in the courtyard, I asked them what they thought. They always gave me a thumbs up sign.

That's what I told the English couple. I also told them that the Doria Pamphilj is reputedly the largest privately-owned museum in Italy and that the family—which, because of intermarriage and adoption, is now more English than Italian—still resides in part of the palazzo. Among the prize possessions, I said, are three Caravaggios and works by Hans Memling, Filippo Lippi, and Titian—plus an even more impressive work, at least in my mind. More about that shortly.

At Babington's I made no effort at daintiness. I knew what I wanted. I wanted Grand High Tea, "a selection of freshly sliced little sandwiches, a selection of home-made mignon cakes, hot-buttered Scottish scones with strawberry jam and freshly whipped cream [which I skipped], and a choice of a Babington Unique Blend." (I was offered no choice but happily accepted the tea brought to me.) The price was €33—steep for lunch anywhere but absolutely worth it to me.

I told the waitress, "*Ogni volta che vengo a Roma, vengo qui.*" I don't remember ever not going to Babington's when visiting the Eternal City. To me, the tea room is as ageless, and as necessary to visit, as the Forum or the Basilica di San Clemente. I luxuriated in my time there. The conversation with my neighbors was delightful, as was becoming stuffed with food that likely was meant for two.

I stepped outside into a driving rain. It abated in a few minutes but otherwise persisted during my long walk to the Capitoline Museums in Piazza Campidoglio above the Roman Forum. I looked forward to spending a couple of hours in a museum complex I hadn't visited in years, but the long and immobile line for tickets persuaded me to go elsewhere. I decided to heed my own advice and headed for Galleria Doria Pamphilj.

I had told the English couple that, fine as the Caravaggios may be, the prize possession of the gallery is Diego Velazquez's large portrait of the family pope, Innocent X, who reigned for eleven years, dying in 1655. If you have a pope in your family's history, you play him up, even if he lacked a pleasing personality, which seems to have been the case with Innocent. He was known as a hard taskmaster, and that comes across in the portrait.

He is seated in a chair, his forearms resting lightly, and is dressed in a silky red mozzetta over a lacy white alb. (Today's white cassock had not yet become de rigueur.) The red of his cape manages to stand out against the red of the chair's back and the deeper red of the draped wall. In his left hand Innocent holds a folded paper. On his right hand is a black ring. His wide mouth is a curveless line. He is seated in three-quarter profile, and his dark eyes are turned directly at the viewer. He seems about to say something unpleasant. When the pope at last saw the finished portrait, he is said to have exclaimed *"Troppo vero!"* ("Too true!"), but that probably isn't a true story. A truer story may be a similar one, that when his servants first saw the portrait, they recoiled in fear because it looked too much like the Innocent they knew.

The most curious thing about the portrait today is its location. You might expect, given its importance to the Pamphilj family, that the portrait would have pride of place in the gallery, that it might have to itself a large room where it could be shown off, much as is done with the *Mona Lisa* at the Louvre. But not so.

I suspect many people tour the entire gallery and never see the Velazquez. The halls of the gallery are chock-a-block with paintings and sculptures, and a surcharge to the ticket will get you entrance also to the Pamphilj apartments, but to see Innocent X's portrait you have to walk into a closet. Or so it seems. Two long corridors meet at a right angle. At the angle is a small room. Perhaps at one time it was a janitor's closet. Today the door is missing. From a distance, down one of the corridors, you see that the room holds a bust. It is of Innocent X and is by Bernini. In fact, it is one of two of that pope by Bernini, both being in Galleria Doria Pamphilj. You can admire the bust—which has no label identifying either the subject or the sculptor—from outside the room. If you go no further, you miss the gallery's prize possession.

If you step into the room to get a closer look at the marble Innocent, as you turn around to your left to exit you are startled to find, in an alcove, the large portrait, so close to you that the pope seems life-size, though that isn't really so. You are as startled as his servants must have been, though in a different way. You are startled at the portrait's sudden appearance and then, after a moment's hesitation, at the realization that it has been positioned here precisely to give you a start. It's a wonderful effect.

On my entering the gallery, and on my exiting, I paused in the small gift shop. I examined mugs which featured some of the gallery's best-known works, but I passed on them. At home we have lots of mugs. On an earlier visit to the museum I had picked up a reproduction of a delightful painting by Peter Brueghel the Younger. It's a copy of a painting done by his father. The title is *Winter Landscape with Skaters and a Bird Trap*. It's one of those finely-wrought Flemish works showing highly-detailed micro-scopic people engaged in everyday activities.

For a reason I no longer remember, I came under the impression that the scene was the elder Brueghel's notion of what winter looked like in the average Italian village. I delighted in such a misconception, since there are no Italian villages in which the main street or square ices over enough to support ice skating. Probably, though, I was misinformed, much as Rick Blaine (Humphrey Bogart) revealed himself to have been when questioned by Captain Renault (Claude Rains):

> "What in heaven's name brought you to Casablanca?"
> "My health. I came to Casablanca for the waters."
> "The waters? What waters? We're in the desert."
> "I was misinformed."

On the way back to my hotel, which was not far from Termini Station, I paid an obligatory visit to the minor basilica dedicated to Santa Prassede. It's just across the street and around the corner from the better known major basilica Santa Maria Maggiore. I think of all Rome's churches Santa Prassede is my favorite. It isn't unknown to tourists, but I never have found it crowded with tourists, and a Sunday Mass there is just that—a Mass—without gaggles of tourists milling around oblivious to the sacred rite.

Santa Prassede is entered normally through a side door. Its main door, located around the far corner on a narrow street, is usually locked. When unlocked, you enter first into a courtyard, the sides of which are regular apartments, and then you pass into the nave of the church. (There used to be a fine bakery to the left of the main door, but it seems to have gone to its heavenly reward. My wife and I once spent two weeks in a fifth-floor apartment at the end of a neighboring street—from the large terrace we had a grand view of the Colosseum—and each morning we would head for the bakery, as good a one as I ever came across in Italy.)

Santa Prassede dates back to the fifth century, but the current edifice was constructed under Pope Pascal I from 817-824. The apse is filled with marvelous mosaics. There are saints everywhere, and standing high up and off to the left is Pope Pascal. The saints have halos, and he has one too, but theirs are round and his is square, signaling that he still was alive when the apse was decorated. As fine as the apse mosaics are, they are distant from the viewer. In a side chapel, dedicated to St. Zenon, you nearly can touch them. The vault of the tiny chapel is filled with mosaics that have a golden background. The images are brilliantly vivid, as though they were made yesterday. To the side, in a yet smaller room, is found a large glass reliquary containing the base and the lower portion of the pillar against which Christ is said to have been scourged. It was brought to Rome from Jerusalem in 1223, the same year in which the fresco of St. Francis of Assisi was painted at Subiaco's Sacro Speco.

The minor basilica saw its share of in-house saints. Cyril

and Methodius, the brothers known as the apostles to the Slavs, lived at Santa Prassede for a while, and Charles Borromeo and Robert Bellarmine, when named cardinals, had this assigned as their titular church. They could have done worse. Mosaics are not commonly found in the churches of Rome, which seems to have favored frescoes, and many say (and I agree with them) that the only finer mosaics are to be found in Ravenna.

So this was my obligatory "churchy" stop in Rome, Babington's having been my obligatory culinary stop. Rome has innumerable places to have tea and probably even more churches, but these two I always visit. Having seen them both and done my duty, I returned to my hotel.

The next morning I was early to the breakfast room and ate standing, just enough to get myself comfortably to the airport. I had done most of my packing the night before, stuffing everything into my backpack, with my filled day pack on top—what I would need on the flight and to get on the flight—and, immediately under it, the duffel bag that would hold the backpack, which had to go as checked luggage because of the trekking poles, which are forbidden as carry-ons. I made sure the Gucci wallet I had purchased for my wife was in the day pack. I trusted the airport's baggage workers not to make off with the books or religious articles that would remain in the backpack, but my trust ended where the Gucci began. It, along with my three essentials (passport, wallet, and phone), would need to stay with me for the duration.

The duration was longer than any of us had expected. The incoming flight was delayed twenty minutes—an inconvenience but not a problem. It still would leave me plenty of time to go through customs and change planes in Charlotte. Once the plane was cleaned it was discovered that there was a problem with the passenger door. I waited for word that the flight would be canceled and that we would be free to scramble for lodgings in Fiumicino or environs, but the word that came was good. We could board. The engines were started, we were towed back from the gate, and we moved forward a short distance—and then stopped, for an interminably long time. The captain got on the intercom and explained that our full flight was too heavy and that we'd have to burn off fuel to achieve proper take-off weight. That took another half hour and, I suppose, wasted hundreds or thousands of dollars' worth of Jet A. (Why didn't they shut down the engines and have the fuel trucks come out and siphon off the excess?)

GRATITUDE

IN THE INTRODUCTION to his guidebook Simone Frignani wrote, "The benefits of the journey are immediate: on the first day you feel euphoric, on the second day you become sociable, and from the third day on you rediscover the pleasure of talking with others." In my case, that's not quite what happened. On the first day, walking out of Norcia, I didn't feel so much euphoric as relieved that I had reached the starting point despite thunderstorms over Dallas. On the second day I had no chance to become sociable with other pilgrims because I saw no other pilgrims and wouldn't see any for several days thereafter. And it would be after the third day that I rediscovered (not that I had lost it) "the pleasure of talking with others," which came first at my lodgings and only later while walking with other hikers.

Simone added, "I would consider my work a failure if someone completed the journey without experiencing an inner change: the journey's purpose is to restore us, step by step, into new men and women." Was I restored by journey's end? Did I experience an inner change? These are not easy questions to answer, except superficially. By the time I got home, I hardly felt restored. I felt exhausted from the tedious return flight. I felt no unmistakable inner change, but inner changes that count are subtle and often aren't recognized until much time has passed. At some point you perceive a change—for good or ill—and look back and think *Yes, that's where it happened; that's what caused it.*

I look at the guidebook's overview map. The Cammino di San Benedetto is a crescent moon through the Apennines. I don't remember now if I had heard of any of the towns it meets before learning about the route. Perhaps I had heard of Norcia and Rieti, but, if so, they were just names. Subiaco? I must have heard of it, knowing something about St. Benedict. Montecassino? I knew the outlines of the story of its destruction during World War II, but I had no real knowledge of it either. Before leaving home I read up on each of the places along the Cammino, though about the smallest places I could find little. It was not until I walked into, through, and out of them that I began to have a sense of them—and a desire to revisit all of them and to linger in some of them.

The Apennines I had known of for decades. How could anyone reading Italian history not know of them? They are the topographic backbone of the Italian peninsula. I spent two weeks walking through the Apennines, coming to appreciate them for what they are and what, over so many centuries, they were in the life and development of a culture to which I long have been drawn. I have no blood relationship to Italy. I am not descended from Italian immigrants to America. If I were, I might apply for dual citizenship, not as a sign of disloyalty to the country of my birth but as a sign of appreciation of a country central to my cultural heritage. All roads lead to Rome—and, in my eyes, from

Rome to Rocca Sinibalda, Orvinio, Castel di Tora, and the other places where I found bigheartedness and camaraderie.

St. Benedict left us no account of his travels, and his pope-biographer, St. Gregory the Great, gave us only the barest outline of where the monk spent time: Norcia, Rome, Subiaco, Montecassino. Local traditions say Benedict's sojourns took him to other places along the Cammino. We fairly can infer his stopping at still other locations along the route, but details of his travels are obscure and forever must remain so. No matter. His spirit infuses the whole area. His name is commemorated in every town, no matter the size. He was a man of contemplation but also a man of action. He built, he taught, he counseled, he prayed, and, like us, he walked. When I passed under Trevi Arch I had a moral certainty that Benedict had passed under it too; after all, it was on the ancient route that led from Subiaco to Montecassino. When I entered Arpino I was confident that Benedict had seen its Roman predecessor, Arpinum, for surely he would have wanted to see the town of Cicero's birth. As I hiked up and down forested hillsides, I knew that Benedict had seen the arboreal ancestors of the trees that gave me shade.

Did my journey effect an inner change? The jury is still out on that. Unlike many, I had not hiked to "find myself" because I had no sense that I had lost myself. At my age—well past the midpoint of life—one doesn't expect major transformations. If you pass forty without knowing who you are, you likely never will know. If you pass forty without having settled principles and ideas, you have wasted at least two decades.

I did not expect a sea change. I did not expect to return home "a different man." I did expect to return home a grateful man, and I think that is what happened. I am grateful for the many kind people I came across along the Cammino di San Benedetto. I am grateful that my hike, though it had its disappointments, reached a happy conclusion. I am grateful simply for having had the chance to go.

Printed in Great Britain
by Amazon

66111332R00124